M000289840

dream homes *country*
100 inspirational interiors

dream homes *country*
100 inspirational interiors

Andreas von Einsiedel

Johanna Thornycroft

MERRELL
LONDON • NEW YORK

For Orlando, Gwendolen and Robin,
and remembering Evelyn

Dream Homes Country is not intended to be a guide to the latest architectural or decorating trends. This collection of country interiors is a celebration of individualism, and what shines through is a passion for colour and collecting, for restoration and rejuvenation, for real log fires and hospitable kitchens. Above all, perhaps, this book illustrates the timelessness of a dream country home and the pleasure offered by such a home both to its owners and to those who simply look and admire.

Those who favour purely contemporary design may argue that traditional country style is, or should be, a thing of the past. Why look back when the future is so exciting? Yet it is interesting to see that the best of the interior-design and decoration magazines have never stopped publishing features on wonderful country houses worldwide, and that is because people want to see them.

Country-style decoration reached a frenzied apogee in the 1970s and 1980s, spreading from cottages and country houses into cities and suburbs around the world. It was instantly recognizable in the lavish use of patterned, usually floral, fabrics, often trimmed with rich fringing and frills, which were applied to curtains, cushions and upholstery alike. Wall-to-wall carpet designs were adapted from archive sources and re-coloured, traditional needlepoint rugs proliferated and faded oriental carpets were spread over coir and rush matting or highly polished floorboards. Pictures were closely grouped, filling every wall; and antiques, from simple Irish pine cupboards to fine Georgian mahogany and early oak, were in great demand.

Although sometimes used to excess, country style had, and retains, a deep resonance. The promise of old-fashioned comfort and relaxation, warmth and, above all, a (real or imagined) slower pace of life continues to be highly attractive. Yet not all country-house owners have relied on multiple patterns and colours to express themselves. Neutral colour schemes have always had an appeal for some, while others believe that white decor best suits their particular house and lifestyle. The thread that links such a diverse range of interiors may be seen as a process of acquisition that is evolutionary and largely unselfconscious. Mismatched dining-room chairs work perfectly in the country, less so in a modern urban space; home-grown flowers displayed in old bottles and jars fit the country scene, whereas florists' creations set the trends in town.

Of the 100 homes featured in this book, the most poignant are probably two Russian dachas (nos. 11 and 33). Barely altered in more than fifty years, these flimsy wooden structures nevertheless provide their owners with not only a refuge from the city but also a palpable connection to the 'happier' times of the past. Like the old cottages of Britain, Europe and the United States, they are country houses where generations recycled whatever they had – the look being usually dictated, rather than designed, principally by climate and limited resources.

The desire to move from the town to the country is, if anything, more popular today than ever before. Although farmhouses have been detached from their farms over the years, cottages sometimes swallowed up by urban development and larger houses often converted into flats, a powerful sense of country remains, with gardens and views across fields or woods playing a major role. City dwellers often move to a country house in order to gain space and privacy and to lead a more natural life, and sometimes simply to sample the joy of living in a quirky old house without close neighbours; so much the better if one's dream home dates from the mid-seventeenth or eighteenth century, contains original chimney pieces or panelling and extra-wide floorboards, and has enough spare bedrooms for some to be converted into luxury en-suite bathrooms.

In warm climates things are different, but not radically so. A Spanish country house may be a gleaming white structure displaying influences from North Africa, but the interior will be furnished with traditional wooden chairs and tables, and there will be a large fireplace, local pottery and decorative tiles. In Italy, colour schemes of faded oxblood and ochre will echo the landscape; materials are terracotta and stone; but here, too, wooden chests and tables will be kept simple. North America displays numerous European influences but has developed a recognizable country style, making use of wraparound verandas and clapboard exteriors, with wood-lined interiors featuring rag rugs and exquisite quilting. Provençal style, with its gently shifting nuances, has had a great impact on country-house decoration, as have the cool, light-filled interiors of Scandinavia.

Most countries have a tradition of painting all manner of surfaces and furniture, and the faded blues, greys and whites common in Sweden and Denmark, and the taupes and beiges of Belgium, inspired by Dutch Old Master paintings, have had a profound influence on contemporary colour schemes. Yet there are no fixed rules. Smaller houses generally benefit from a single colour scheme, which expands the sense of space in living-rooms. Larger houses may take advantage of a wider colour spectrum – from deep-red or dark-blue dining-rooms, brightly painted kitchens and wall-papered drawing-rooms to delicate pastels in bedrooms; the choice often depends on the period of the house, and when it comes to 'document' wallpaper, there is a vast array of options.

Fashion impacts less, or certainly more slowly, on country-house interior design than on that of the city. That is not to say that country houses are not sophisticated, but rather that, for country homes, people usually prefer traditional elements, such as well-made inter-lined curtains, cosseting four-poster beds with wool or cashmere blankets, and wide, down-filled sofas. The rooms are likely to have retained decorative mouldings and period fireplaces, now missing from so many city apartments, so owners tend to choose furnishings that fit well with the existing original elements.

One of the joys of owning a country house is the pleasure of seeking out, for example, old china and jugs, antique blankets or kitchen baskets, odd lengths of fabric and old curtains; finding a suitably dented pewter candlestick that is just right for the kitchen table may be deemed a triumph. The idea of such collecting, by no means new, is to create a latter-day 'Grand Tour' impression: eclectic assemblies of items from around the world, such as Chinese pots and lamp bases, kelims from Turkey and Morocco, textiles from Uzbekistan and strange, alluring tribal art from Africa or the Pacific. Country-house owners generally never stop looking for interesting things; books arrive on shelves, chairs and tabletops as if by magic. Every generation brings its own twist to a family home. The Cape Dutch homestead (no. 21) is a terrific example of successive generations of one family adding furniture and decorative objects to a house that absorbs and welcomes everything within it. It is impossible to create such interior decoration in a short space of time.

Perhaps the greatest change to country style has come about through greater public knowledge, gained from television programmes and from the huge number of books available about restoring old houses and period decoration. In the last decade or so there has been an explosion of

interest in using 'historic' paint colours, and it is no longer necessary to mix one's own paint (although some designers still do so). Established businesses, such as Papers and Paints in London, have flourished, manufacturing eco-friendly paint and offering advice on historic colours that have been used over centuries, often based on local pigments and therefore specific to a given region.

While a Tuscan villa, a Provençal bastide or a perfectly proportioned Georgian country house may remain classic aspirations, converted barns, stables and other isolated farm buildings are bringing the country dream within easier reach, to more people. An unfitted, inefficient, although charming kitchen may be replaced by Bulthaup or Boffi; bathrooms may increase in number, size and comfort; but still the essential mix of inherited furniture and pictures, favourite junk-shop finds and modern art remains a defining feature of country style. Such a mix reveals not only our continued penchant for possessions and the desire for self-expression but also a love of visual stimulus – one that does not necessarily mean clutter.

By its very nature, a dream country home should be welcoming and sociable, even if muddy boots and damp dogs are not part of the scene. A country house is a flexible, multi-functioning dwelling, where the emphasis, even in cooler climates, is on both indoor and outdoor living. Historically, when people made money they built a new country house; now, unsurprisingly, numerous people want to buy and decorate an old one. Of many splendid examples illustrated here, home no. 32 is a wonderful glimpse of a complex restoration where, among the many discoveries hidden behind plasterboarding, were fine Gothic stone architectural details, which were cleaned and brought back to life. The owners decorated every room, taking their guide from existing elements, from the original plasterwork to the size of the windows. A love of Classicism and French style combined with an instinctive skill in the use of 'modern' paint colours has resulted in a tour de force of revival.

While fashion and interior design move on apace, it is in the country house that we find some of the last bastions of the familiar, nostalgic scenes from the past – sometimes romantic, sometimes shabby and sometimes very grand. A large country house remains a status symbol; a smaller one is something to which countless people may aspire.

1 To the manor

Local people still remember the time when this house near Saint-Rémy-de-Provence was a café and local meeting place, although it was originally a small farmhouse, built in the 1820s. A major restoration and development project was undertaken some years ago, with an Aix-en-Provence designer advising on all aspects of the house and garden. Taking account of local architectural tradition, the owners expanded the property by raising both ends of the house high above the old roofline, creating a dramatic hall, lit by a double-height window. From here, an impressive stone-and-iron staircase provides the primary access to the first floor. Among the many exceptional qualities of the house, from its extraordinary front garden to the flowing layout of its rooms, several elements stand out. The ground floor has been laid with reclaimed eighteenth-century Burgundy limestone flagstones, while upstairs the floors are made of planed and sanded oak boards, giving a dry, matt finish of great beauty. Antique stone fireplaces grace all the principal rooms, and the core of the old house retains its gigantic fireplace in the original kitchen. All the furniture has been selected with great attention to age, style and quality. Double layers of neutral Belgian linen filter sunlight through the windows.

2 Metamorphosis

The search for a perfect country house can be a drawn-out and soul-destroying business. A young London-based couple had to look for a long time before they eventually discovered this classic William and Mary house in south-west England. They instantly decided to buy it, despite knowing that it would mean living within a work-in-progress for several years. Windows had to be replaced, services installed and bathrooms created; life was initially lived mostly in the kitchen and the living-room, which were in reasonable condition. Having grown up with a mother who taught her interior-design skills from a young age, and also having worked in fashion, the wife gradually turned this unloved old house into an exquisite family home. From the cool, uncluttered hall with its original stone floors, the rooms open up to reveal a palette of soft and subtle colours. Furnishings are a mix of inherited antiques and paintings and a young, fresh take on country style that incorporates simple tongue-and-groove panelling, sisal carpets, checked cottons and toiles de Jouy. The talented owner–designer has worked with the fabric of the building to allow the sense of proportion and age to shine through.

3 Flower power

Childhood memories and a love of sunshine and flowers inspired the choice of colours and fabrics in the restoration of this clapboard house in Connecticut as a vacation home. All the woodwork in the welcoming kitchen, dominated by a large fireplace, has been painted a strong Mediterranean blue – a colour echoed in the blue-and-white plates hanging on the white walls above. The perfect complement to blue is yellow, introduced into this interior by means of a large painting by Roger Mühl. Identifying pastels as her particular favourite for fabrics, the owner, a designer and writer on lifestyle subjects, has chosen a flower-patterned pink, blue and white chintz for the living-room sofas. White walls and bare floorboards add a light and summery touch to the decorative theme, and the owner's choice of country chairs and tables suits the cottage architecture perfectly. In the master bedroom upstairs, flower paintings, fresh garden flowers and quilts featuring flowers blend surprisingly well with the pink, yellow and green floral bed hangings. The key to the success of the interior design is in the choice of complementary pastel colours.

4 Rescue and revival

It takes imagination and courage to turn a run-down group of Provençal buildings into a dream home, let alone find them in the first place, given the popularity of Provence as an international holiday destination where ownership is prized above renting. From the start, the owner could visualize renovating this mid-1850s house, which is at the edge of a village, to fulfil her desire for open-plan summer and winter living. The kitchen and expansive ground-floor reception rooms were created by removing part of the existing stone dividing walls and inserting broad arches instead. Right across the front, French windows can be opened to blur the boundary between the interior and the full-width limestone terrace. The house contained some welcome secrets, revealed only after layers of plasterboard had been stripped out: wonderfully distressed beams, a grand fireplace and distinctive stonework indicated that the original builder had been a man of some means. A major element of the works included building the interior of the barn, which now houses the master bedroom. The garden, formerly just a car park, has been transformed, and now at its centre is an enormous black swimming pool, edged in stone and surrounded by fruit trees, roses, clematis and a wall of bamboo.

5 Cotswold colonial

The Cotswolds in south-west England is one of the most beautiful areas in the country, and many people dream of owning a centuries-old stone house or cottage in one of the region's numerous small villages surrounded by rolling farmland and streams. While this cottage looks very old, it was in fact built in the 1950s. The owner, a New Zealander who works in London, had trained in law before moving to a career in interior design, and inevitably sought a bolthole away from his busy city life. Very little maintenance had been undertaken, but the cottage was structurally sound. Although much of the furniture was bought in New Zealand, the interiors are decorated in a restrained but nonetheless English country style, made more casual than usual by means of, for example, setting cane chairs around a circular library/dining table, using less patterned fabric than normal and having no busy groups of pictures or china. Living in the country is often as much about the garden as the house, and here only the simplest of curtains adorns the windows, letting plenty of light into the rooms and allowing the garden almost to come indoors.

6 Tuscan belle

Set four-square in the rich agricultural lands of eastern Tuscany, this eighteenth-century farmhouse has been restored by a Belgian artist and designer to become a multi-family holiday home. The house had been uninhabited for years and was almost derelict. A two-year restoration programme was undertaken, in which careful preservation was the main objective. A loggia runs across the front, facing fields and a range of blue–green hills in the distance. The ground floor, formerly cattle barns, houses a large kitchen, a bedroom off the hallway and, down one side, an exotic 'Turquerie', which has been created with hand-painted fabrics and wall decorations. An enormous fireplace dominates the first floor, which would originally have been the kitchen. Now the room is used as a sitting-room, which is cool in summer and warm in winter. There are numerous bedrooms, each one differently but simply decorated in soft, faded colours. All bathrooms are the same, varying only in shape and size. The designer and her architect worked in complete accord, one complementing the other, and at the project's completion nothing appears to be new and intervention seems minimal.

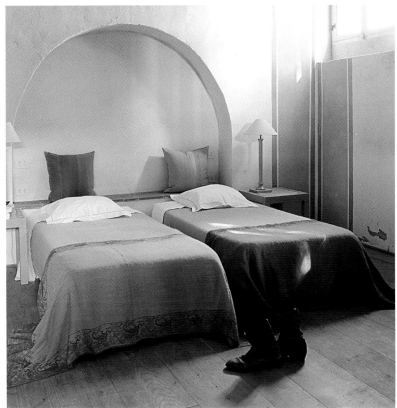

7 Art de vivre

There is a remarkable story attached to this classical eighteenth-century stone house, formerly a hunting lodge, near Aix-en-Provence. It was originally built some 130 kilometres (80 miles) away, near Carpentras, by an archbishop of Avignon. The present owner bought it as a ruin and moved it stone by stone to its present rural site and rebuilt it, during which process he also created a complex garden of great beauty. He added projecting wings to the existing house, one of which is a living-room, the other the kitchen. The original house is decorated and furnished in *ancien régime* style, the dining-room lined in chinoiserie panels, the bedrooms lavishly swathed in fabrics from Braquenié. The new living-room, however, was inspired in part by Moroccan interiors and features red-and-white-striped linen banquette seating and stools, with the walls covered in the same Belgian fabric, and the whole anchored by a colourful oriental carpet. The several animal and polo studies are by artist Aurelian Raynaud. The old-fashioned kitchen appears ancient, with its stone sinks and painted cupboards lined with linen; a sixteen-seat table surrounded by country chairs creates a timeless tableau. House and garden, created by a man who is internationally renowned for his style, are the embodiment of all that is promised by French country living.

8   Island idyll

The island of St Lucia in the Caribbean is a great place to build a dream home. The many hilly sites afford superb views of the sea, and the climate ensures that any garden becomes a bountiful and colourful tropical splendour. The owner of this house on the coast was inspired to commission its building by his chosen architect's own home in Barbados. The owner's mother, an experienced designer of Caribbean interiors, was on hand to advise on the choice of colour, furniture and decoration, ever mindful of the need for simplicity. Open walkways, guarded by wooden pillars and handrails, curve around the site, allowing cooling sea breezes to penetrate the rooms. The open-beamed ceilings look appropriately casual, and almost everything is white: built-in seating and much of the furniture are painted white, and white fabrics have been used for cushions and on the beds. The only colour to be seen, apart from the natural wood tones of the bedsteads and some carved Asian furniture, is a riot of yellow-and-blue tiling in the bathroom, shiny copper pans in the kitchen and blue-and-white table-settings.

9 Natural charm

An English family returning from the United States bought this eighteenth-century Cotswold mill house and set about a programme of modernization with the help of a local architectural designer. Inspired by the designer's own conversion of an old stable block, the new owners were confident she understood their requirements. The work was described as 'pulling a large period building to pieces in order to impose a better layout'. The owners and designer were in complete accord, working together to accommodate a collection of contemporary art and an extensive library. The mill ceased functioning in the 1940s, although the millstone and grinding gear have remained in place; because the spaces are so large, the machinery, which rises from the dining-room through the library above, neither dominates nor appears twee. The expansive living spaces are decorated in calm, earthy colours and largely plain or subdued fabrics from such suppliers as Claremont, Percheron and Fortuny. The furniture is a mix of American and English antiques and modern large-scale sofas. All eight bedrooms are decorated in true country style, while the kitchen is the heart of the home, with a large Aga cooker, aged oak units, stone floors and original structural beams. With a magnificent Albertine rose covering the mellow stone façade, this is truly a rural idyll.

10 Budget beauty

The idea of moving to a lovely old house in France can be driven as much by a desire for increased space as by a quest for a complete change of lifestyle – as was the case with this pretty eighteenth-century house in the Lot-et-Garonne region. The young Anglo-American owner took on much of the restoration work herself, including creating a workshop where she designs and makes lampshades. The cheapest way of updating interiors is to paint them, and in old French houses white, pale blue, grey or muted greens work particularly well. Many original features of this house have survived, from the wobbly flagstone floors and wooden staircase to doors and windows and, of course, the irregular beams. Each room has a distinctive character. An abstract stencil pattern in red has been applied to one of the bedroom walls, creating an effect that is more casual than wallpaper; the red-and-white theme is taken up in headboards covered in floral fabric. A lovely antique crystal chandelier and a decorated curtain pelmet bring touches of grandeur to the dining-room. Inexpensive oriental rugs add colour and warmth to the floors, and comfortable old armchairs have simply had single pieces of fabric draped on the seats and large cushions placed in the backs.

11 1950s nostalgia

This simple wooden dacha in a forest outside St Petersburg in Russia was given to the owner's grandfather, Abraham Fyodorovich Joffe, by Joseph Stalin in 1947. Joffe was an internationally acclaimed scientist, known as the Father of Soviet physics, and as such was presented with a summer house that had not only water and electricity laid on but also the luxury of a chauffeur's cottage. The contents are largely original, including a MIR television made in 1954 and a 'Leningrad' fridge of 1955. There are traditional tiled stoves in every room, and the Lincrusta- (textured wallpaper) lined walls are insulated with coal dust. Brown linoleum is nailed neatly on to the floorboards in an effort to stop draughts. The sense of being in a time warp is powerful, and although some painting has been carried out over the years, the atmosphere is pure 1950s in every detail, from the fabrics and light fittings to the bathroom and the kitchen. Every weekend the owner and her mother and daughter travel by train from the city and walk to their dacha, but all around them is a building boom; the old style is no longer popular. The gardens and forest so beloved of earlier generations are fast disappearing.

12 French polish

That rarefied part of Provence known as the 'Golden Triangle' (between Avignon, Arles and Aix-en-Provence) is filled with exceptionally beautiful homes, many with large, superbly designed gardens, of which this is a perfect example. The owners of these properties come from Paris, northern Europe, the United States and beyond. Rarely are the farmhouses, or *mas*, as they are known, in sufficiently good condition to satisfy the desires of the new owners. Specialist firms in the region, with intimate knowledge of restoration techniques, now bring back to life many of the semi-ruined *mas* and bastides. Usually built of limestone, they were originally the houses and barns that formed the hub of farming communities, and the best restoration programmes make use of traditional methods and materials. Attached barns become drawing-rooms, tractor sheds make orangeries, and often a new staircase has to be built to reach the upper floors. So skilful is much of the work that it is barely possible to tell what is original and what is new. Window glass appears old, floor- and wall-tiles are reclaimed and carefully selected for patina, fireplace surrounds are bought second-hand, and walls are finished in traditional colours. It is a style that is much copied throughout the world but is never quite as good as the real thing.

13 Kentish character

Anyone unfamiliar with the oast houses of southern England must wonder why such strange-looking places were built. Circular brick structures topped with conical kilns and cowls, they were used for drying hops, a major ingredient in the brewing of beer. As hop-farming declined, these curious buildings have been converted into spacious country homes, although the rounded walls always create a design challenge, especially where a fitted kitchen is installed. In this group of oasts, the bedrooms are on the ground floor, while the spacious living areas above – the sitting-room is some 12 metres (40 ft) long – make the most of the wonderful countryside views. With forests of structural beams playing a major role in each of the rooms, the decoration has been limited to a range of white tones for the walls, floors, upholstery and kitchen work surfaces. While rich, warm colours remain popular for country-house decoration, white is the perfect foil for timber and stone and the myriad shades of brown country furniture, from the palest pine to deep mahogany and oak. The owner has chosen a good mix of modern sofas and antique tables and chairs. Enormous bunches of country flowers in overscaled glass vases add an appropriate dash of colour and scent in the living- and dining-rooms.

14 American classic

Columbia County, north of New York City, contains a wealth of historic architecture, including numerous nineteenth-century houses that have retained their integrity despite often being on the verge of collapse. An artist and restorer, who makes no distinction between fine and applied arts, undertook this renovation in the spirit of the 1820s Federal style, rather than trying to re-create absolute period detailing. The layout is typical of the date, with a good central hall and a four-over-four configuration. All the essential services had to be renewed; walls, floors and ceilings were stripped and redecorated; and the bathrooms and kitchen were all replaced. Although the palette is neutral, the owner has applied various painting techniques to give the impression of aged painted surfaces: broken whites, bleached floorboards and scraped-back pressed-tin ceilings that are left with a mottled finish. Furniture and *objets d'art* span the Neo-classical, Regency and Biedermeier periods, chosen for their strong presence and simple, functional design. There are collections of old photographs, African masks and plaster busts, and plenty of books. Little colour has been used; the interior relies instead on natural textures and changing light levels.

15 Holiday home

Finding the ideal holiday home can take a great deal of time and often involves making a compromise between old and new – a compromise that, in this case, has been triumphantly achieved. The core of this now delightful residence on the island of Mallorca was a small farmhouse without running water or electricity, but the property had some land attached to it, wonderful views and plenty of potential. The new owners called on an interior designer who had worked with them on a previous home. A low-tech restoration was planned, encompassing the original small house, a right-angled addition and the conversion of two separate barns. One barn has become a guest house, the other an office. The new wing is barely distinguishable from the old; it appears to have evolved rather than to have been built deliberately. The use of traditional materials was an important feature. Beamed ceilings, whitewashed walls, old Mallorcan tiles and practical latticed wooden doors in the kitchen, along with small traditional windows and tiled floors, create a convincing sense of age. The interiors are simple, casual, pretty and summery, although the large fireplaces are often in use during the winter.

16 New look

The American owners of this small French country house employed an English architectural practice based near Les Baux in Provence to enlarge and restore an old smithy, or forge. Because of strict planning rules, the footprint of existing structures had to be followed, which meant that innovative design was required to create a cohesive whole from what was a series of lean-to spaces attached to the house. A lofty single-storey addition turned the original small, square house into a much more spacious home. The new room houses a compact contemporary kitchen, and dining and living area, and gives on to a largely glass winter room facing the garden. Upstairs in the old house are two luxurious bedrooms and bathrooms, while below is a further living-room and a small study. Along the back of the house is a flexible space comprising a library-cum-guest suite and a covered dining terrace. White floors and walls set off white and cream furniture, with a few antique pieces adding a change of tone. A collection of contemporary art, along with Pueblo Indian pots, provides great interest in this cool, calm and smoothly modern scheme, which so well illustrates how an old house can accommodate up-to-date architectural features.

17 Barn conversion

A photographer with a passion for the Arts and Crafts period, and his wife, an acclaimed artist, have converted an 1840s stone barn in the English Cotswolds into a comfortable home entirely of their own design. The conversion respects the vernacular tradition of the area, and all the materials have been sourced and made up locally. Reclaimed Cotswold stone slabs were laid on the ground floor, wide English elm boards on the upper floors, and a mixture of elm and oak in the kitchen, bathrooms and bedrooms. Every fitting, from window latches to door furniture, and all the light fixtures, were made especially for the house, as was all the wooden furniture. These intrepid builders even opened their own quarry to supply building stone. The walls incorporate traditional horsehair-and-lime plaster; the colours were mixed at home. Adrian Mustoe made the kitchen; Colin Hawkins was responsible for the lighting; and Colin Clark made much of the furniture. Inherited oriental rugs add dashes of colour, but little embellishment is required in this house, where wood and stone provide all the variety of colour and texture needed. The overall effect is not only beautiful but also totally in keeping with the building and its environment.

18 Northern light

Set in rural East Anglia in the east of England, a group of three thatched cottages was converted into one dwelling by its Danish owner. The interiors of the house, and particularly the studio, reflect his love of all things Scandinavian, especially that luminous, soft grey–white that works so well in northern climates. He has not slavishly relied on Danish and Swedish pieces, but the overall impression is that of a country house in Sweden, where French influences in the eighteenth and nineteenth centuries made quite an impact. The house and studio share the same calm and airy aesthetic, a monochrome world but one that is constantly changing with the seasons and varying levels of light. Floorboards, beams and panelled walls are all washed in the same colour; mirrors, chairs, a secretaire and chest are similarly pale. There is little pattern to disturb the serenity – just a checked fabric used on a sofa and chairs, plain gunmetal grey here and there, and a floral stripe on a bedroom chair. Touches of silver, black and gilt punctuate the pale spaces, contrasting beautifully with the quiet grey wash.

19 English style

The Provence-based English architect who worked on the property featured in this book as home no. 16 was asked by his client to rebuild completely and extend this former beekeeper's house near Saint-Rémy-de-Provence. A well-known London-based interior designer, the client was keen to create a holiday home with open, flowing spaces in a modern style, while at the same time retaining any typically French elements, such as structural beams and the windows and shutters, and using the creamy local limestone for floors and outdoor terraces. The house was to be a relaxed and comfortable antidote to the stresses of city living, furnished with large sofas and chairs covered in the owner's own range of colourful and practical striped or patterned fabrics. All the living-rooms have been painted white, with soft lilac, pink and blue being introduced to the bedrooms. A new ground-floor room, facing the pool, was built, housing a white, custom-made kitchen to one side, a dining area in the centre, lined up on an antique fireplace, and a comfortable sitting space beyond. Rooms designed in this way are convivial and social and especially suited to summer living.

20 Artful arrangement

Antiques dealers' homes are likely to reflect their stock in trade, as exemplified by this house in Arundel, West Sussex. A former coaching inn dating from the fifteenth century, it is characterized by an eclectic mix of English and French country furniture and accessories assembled from far and wide. The style is neither town nor country, but the deep sofas, abundance of tables and colourful fabrics put the emphasis on comfort and relaxation. The owners like their treasures to be displayed in a well-organized fashion: pairs are better than singles, and interesting and unusual groupings are created by teaming objects of contrasting size, shape and colour. Old exposed brickwork, ancient timber beams and tiled floors allow for a less rigid scheme than plastered and painted walls would have done. Not everything is antique, however. The dealer's eye for adapting lovely 'bits and pieces' has resulted in the production, for example, of coffee tables using decorative old ironwork. It takes confidence and skill to mix textiles, china, timber and furniture from different periods. Antiques have a way of fitting into almost any interior; it is the way in which they are combined and arranged that reflects twenty-first-century living.

21 Cape classic

To be the owner of an old South African Cape Dutch homestead, set in its own vineyard, is the stuff of dreams. This rare and extraordinary house has been in the same family for hundreds of years, and its contents reflect that fact. It would be impossible to buy, in a single lifetime, the diverse and eclectic range of objects and furniture that fills every room. It is a house that can be read like a book: page after page of the family's history is displayed, from the earliest arrivals, who brought European furniture with them, right up to the present day, as the current owner adds his own choice of pictures, lamps and *objets d'art*. Those bedrooms and bathrooms that are set under the towering thatched roof are quite different from those on the floors below. Each one somehow takes on the character of its materials and varying light levels. Some rooms appear to be entirely European in origin, others very African, especially where furniture has been locally made of native woods rarely seen in Europe. Bold colour is to be found everywhere: red leather, pink and blue velvet, yellow and lime-green stripes, and floral patterns are all juxtaposed; yet nothing bothers the eye. This wonderful house is a compelling cabinet of curiosities.

22 Grand manner

A wonderful mix of English and French styles graces this imposing eighteenth-century bastide, the Provençal holiday home of a couple who, with their family, spend as much time here as they can. Much of the restoration work was undertaken by the premier architectural practice in the region, a family business renowned for its expertise in historical reconstruction and refurbishment. Still retaining some 160 hectares (400 acres) of the original large estate, the property remains a *domaine* (wine producer) and an olive producer. Colefax and Fowler supplied many of the floral and other fabrics, while Lucinda Oakes, an expert decorative painter, worked her magic on numerous rooms. A comfortable, traditional country kitchen is at the heart of the home, with a formal living-room adjacent to it. A cool retreat is provided by the garden room, formerly an old garage, with its white-painted cane chairs and French metal table, and its walls embellished by delicate painted foliage. An equestrian sculpture by Stella Shawzin is perfectly placed on the hall console table and balanced by a pair of painted eighteenth-century chairs and a Classical urn set atop a stone plinth. Outside, the gardens are notable especially for their collection of roses.

23 Original view

An old quarryman's cottage did not initially seem to have much going for it when a young British ceramicist first found it tucked away in the Forest of Dean in south-west England. It was dark, divided into two, had wobbly additions and had been used as a cider house for years – which explains why the doorways are wider than normal (just a little wider than a cider barrel, to be exact). But those of us driven to expend vast amounts of effort on our homes do not worry about small imperfections. This talented owner first lived in the house, getting to know the light levels and how the rooms would work, leading one to another. Anyone who knows the owner's work will not be surprised to see her idea of a dream interior, using as it does the myriad colours and the rose motif seen on her pots, plates, mugs and bowls. Colour is an abiding passion; white is anathema. There are no pictures on the walls, and all the furniture is practical and functional. One must applaud the owner's originality and courage of conviction.

24 Basle beauty

Fine period detailing should be regarded as a bonus in any house, and the great thing about today's attitudes to design is that a host of different styles can be accommodated in an infinite variety of modern interiors. This elegant early nineteenth-century villa near Basle in Switzerland was decorated and furnished by a couple with a wide-ranging knowledge of European style. The most striking features of the house are the beautifully proportioned windows and the fine wood grains of the floors, architraves and doors. While the drawing-room has the appearance of an English country house, with its needlepoint rug, floral curtains and low tables piled with interesting books, the coral-coloured dining-room, with its unusual painted table and chairs, appears to be influenced by French and Swedish styles. Particularly effective are the symmetrical groups of pictures throughout the house and the way in which a collection of majolica plates has been displayed on an old carved shelf unit in the dining area of the small kitchen. A beautiful example of what is usually called 'traditional' interior design, the house feels wonderfully orderly and secure and is a much-loved home.

25 Island character

Leaving the cool climes of northern Europe behind to live in the sun is surely a recurring dream for many people. Those who succeed often find that their lives take a completely new course. The refurbishment of this Mallorcan farmhouse so impressed friends and locals that it led its owners to set up an architecture and design business on the island. Two shops also now supply an international clientele with all manner of antiques, fabrics and furniture, some of which is made to the owners' designs, in both traditional metalwork and wood. The furnishing and decorating of this home set their company's standard for comfortable but casual island living. Mindful of retaining the seventeenth-century character of the house, the owners carefully controlled the modernizing work, but the landscaping of the large property was a major project. As with most old farmhouses, there were barns attached that could be converted into a summer dining-room or seating area. Dark beams, white walls and painted floors are the background against which colourful dhurries and kelims add warmth and texture. A mix of dark European furniture and neutral contemporary sofas creates a relaxed environment, and plenty of vernacular architectural detailing helps convey the essential character of this enviable place in the sun.

26   Light touch

This lovely stone house in Kent, south-east England, dates from 1815 and was given as a wedding gift to the current owner by her father. She was also fortunate enough to inherit a great deal of fine furniture of a similar date to the house – including early Thonet and a collection of Biedermeier – with which she began furnishing the many large rooms. The house is characterized in style by restraint and a certain simplicity, and conservation rather than restoration was the driving force behind its decoration. As a painter herself, the owner was well versed in the language of colour and proportion. Artists often like to buy and display the work of other artists; in the bedroom shown here is a dramatic painting by Stephen Rose. The large family kitchen is set a few steps lower than the entrance hall and was probably once a series of utility rooms; with its five large windows overlooking the 7.5-hectare (19-acre) garden, it became the heart of the house. Years of development with the help of a garden designer have turned the park-like grounds into a pleasure garden of vistas, focal points and carefully planned tree planting. Gradations of innumerable shades of green lead one's eye from the front of the house over a stone-edged pond and beyond.

27 Barnstorm

The sculptural quality of the numerous old oak beams in this former barn was one of the things that attracted the present owner to what she describes as an impulse purchase. Located in rural south-west France, the barn and its adjoining house required three years' restoration work before the owner could move in. The property has a traditional exterior of stone walls and light-blue shutters, but the interiors are markedly different. The kitchen area, once a cattle stall, has the appearance of a weightless white construction that seems barely to touch the timber framework. It is contemporary and practical, designed in such a way that diners cannot see over the countertops to the work area beyond. Set under the rafters in the old hayloft, the master bedroom overlooks the main living area. The subtly varying tones of the timber create a soothing ambience that is kept quiet and calm by the choice of leather furniture, cream and white fabrics and old stone. Very little colour was needed in such a strongly defined architectural space.

28 Provence palette

An American artist who divides her time between Provence and New York bought this property, nudging the old Roman road to Arles, because of the garden rather than the house itself. The garden was brilliantly and lavishly laid out, serving as a wonderful setting for the simple stone house. Over time the lofty cypress trees, clipped yew and box balls became the subjects of a series of admired paper and collage works by the artist. The house, though, was certainly not lacking in charm itself. Once restored, the interiors became a three-dimensional canvas, where the owner layered pigments on to the walls, painted furniture and cupboards and hung coloured curtain fabrics. She has mixed 1930s and 1940s furniture evocative of the Riviera with country Louis XV and XVI, a suite of Napoleon III and gigantic antique mirrors and consoles, creating a harmonious melding of classic and Baroque. Most of the contents were found locally and in the nearby antiques town of L'Isle-sur-la-Sorgue. The owner's own work adorns the walls of nearly every room, some of the pictures being from the 'Cyprès' series painted here, in her studio located between the yellow living-room and an old orangery. The beauty of the house is that it appears to have slowly evolved, furnished by a woman with a natural feeling for country style.

29 Grand design

This fairy-tale castle near Antwerp in Belgium is renowned as the home
and former atelier of Belgium's most respected collector and dealer –
an expert in an extraordinarily diverse range of objects, from early
Egyptian sculpture to Baroque furniture, from simple country tables
and chairs to contemporary art and sculpture. His love and knowledge
of architecture and restoration have attracted commissions for many
projects all over the world. Known simply as 'the castle', this house is
filled with glorious collections spanning many centuries and cultures.
The pure-white dining-room is used to display blue-and-white Ming
china recovered from a shipwreck. Light pours into the orangery
through elegant arched windows, illuminating not only plants and
flowers but also a diverse mixture of furniture, pots and porcelain. Floor
materials are an important part of any interior, and here they include
ancient tiles, waxed timber boards and intricate parquet, softened and
enlivened by many interesting rugs. The library and study are evocative
of the eighteenth and nineteenth centuries; they are characterized by
cabinets of curiosities that are perfectly at ease with modern linen-
covered chairs and sofas. This is no period pastiche. A master of the
art of interior design has created a unique family home.

30   Layers of colour

The 1960s were memorable for many reasons, but the decade is hardly remembered for its architectural brilliance. Although unimpressed with the front of this house in Surrey, southern England, when she first saw it, an interior designer spotted the potential to create a family home in which the main focus of living would be a new kitchen and dining-room, taking advantage of the sunny west-facing garden. The kitchen units were painted yellow, with blue detailing and blue worktops tying in with the blue open-plan dining area. Another of the owner's favourite colour combinations is red and yellow, cheerful and warm in winter and perfect for country living-rooms: here against the yellow wallpaper she has used numerous shades of red for upholstery, cushions and the floral-print curtains, while the lamp bases are blue and white. The room is pulled together by a geometric oriental carpet and a kelim-covered ottoman. The owner chose red again for her own bedroom – classic country choices of a red-and-white toile wallpaper, matching fabric and lampshades, and a traditional brass bed. The style here is all about the confident mixing of fabrics and textures, without carefully colour-matching everything.

31   Caribbean style

Many British colonists, builders and architects incorporated prevailing Victorian fashions into homes far removed from 'dear old England'. Nostalgia played a large part in colonial architecture around the world, from the Caribbean to Australia and New Zealand. In St Lucia particularly, the 'Gingerbread' house — all lacy fretwork verandas, bargeboards and railings — became the traditional style. This fine example of the genre is in fact a late twentieth-century distillation of a great deal of research and planning by both its former and its current owners. Eminently suited to today's lifestyle, the house nonetheless has all the atmosphere and ambience of its historic antecedents. Loft-tray ceilings, hardwood floors and potted palms; blue-and-white china and oriental cupboards and rugs; fine bone china and sugary paint colours — all combine to create a real sense of history. While most of the furniture in the house was bought in St Lucia and Barbados, some pieces, such as the four-poster beds, were designed by the owner and made locally. The tropical gardens are filled with palms and pink bougainvillea, and the southerly views are the stuff of dreams.

32 Gothic revival

Not put off by the daunting nature of the restoration work required, a young couple took on this substantial Victorian rectory and created a place of great beauty. Thirty people worked on the house for eighteen months. Fine Gothic stonework was revealed behind boarded-up walls, but it soon became clear that many additions had been made to an even earlier building. Behind the façade lay the good proportions of a Georgian house. With no professional help, the owners – inspired by influences ranging from Classicism to the French designer Jacques Garcia – undertook the interior decoration themselves. The reception rooms are grouped around an inner staircase hall. Seen from the main entrance to the hall, the combined library and living-room is on the right, opening to a stone corner tower. Painted in colours of 'old rose' and white, the drawing-room occupies the second bay, and beyond it is the dining-room. These rooms are furnished with a mixture of antique furniture, fine fabrics, hand-blocked wallpaper and oriental rugs, as are eight bedroom suites, but on the rear ground floor the mood changes to contemporary for the more private spaces. Bulthaup supplied the kitchen, and solid blocks of wall colour set off the mostly modern furniture in the living-rooms opposite.

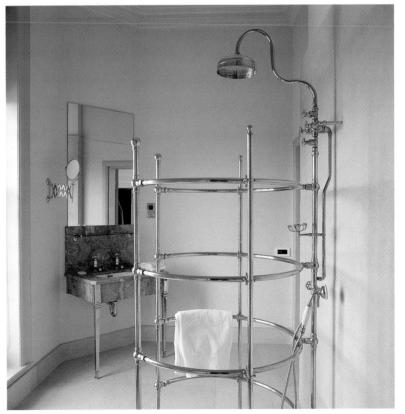

33 Times past

A dacha, for Russians, is far more than just a summer holiday cottage. Popular as retreats in the nineteenth century, dachas gained favour once more after World War II, with many being built by the regime as gifts for favoured scientists and politicians. In a vast country of long, harsh winters and short, light summers, the dacha embodies an idealized romantic past when families swam in the lakes and took tea around the samovar, when wild mushrooms were gathered in the forests, wildflowers picked, and berries and vegetables harvested and preserved. Many post-war and earlier examples survive. Here, on the Gulf of Finland, is a typical vernacular timber house built on granite foundations by the owner's grandfather in 1955. There is no running water and no real 'interior decoration' as it is commonly considered; there was very little money to improve or change anything. The contents are largely original, bought second-hand or by the coupon system, but the rooms are filled with paintings by the owner and her sister. One or two pre-Revolution pieces survived the upheaval of 1918. Local women crochet cushions and still sell traditional needlework; the straw chairs date to the 1950s. The owner and her family spend every summer in this charming little house with its wild garden.

34 Decorative sympathy

To own a country house or cottage is an enduring and romantic dream for many people. Whether the property is a converted barn or an old stable block, located in a forest or a field, setting and original purpose do not seem to matter as long as it is in the countryside. But such a home is difficult to find in many countries. The owner of this 200-year-old cottage in northern Germany is well aware of its rarity value. Found through word of mouth and previously owned by a couple who had similar decorative sympathies, this house required little work to create exactly what the new owner wanted from her weekend and holiday retreat. The roof was re-thatched, a shower room added and the whole place painted in the pale colours that reflect its location near the Danish border. Paint has been used to transform not only the interior but also most of the furniture: bought for shape and function, regardless of condition, it is all painted in the Scandinavian colours so beloved of its artistic chatelaine. This cottage has it all: a quiet agricultural location, sweeping views, a large pond and a garden that is developing into a cottage classic.

35 Reviving tradition

When the current owners first saw it, this eighteenth-century Provençal farmhouse appeared almost derelict. Modern partitions had been used to carve up the interiors into boxlike spaces, and it was hard to tell how the original house had been laid out. However, the owners, both designers, had plenty of experience of renovating old dwellings, and once all the superfluous layers had been removed, it was clear to them that they had acquired a gem. They planned to create a traditional French house – perhaps a little grander than a farmer might have aspired to, but one that would provide year-round comfort in a region of dramatic variations in seasonal temperatures. Warm, earthy colours were chosen to complement the terracotta floor-tiles. Stone fireplaces, painted *trompe l'œil* panelling and faux-marble skirting boards were used to set the scene. Period detailing was emphasized throughout. Cupboard doors have been lined with pleated fabric; china is displayed on open shelving; and there is an eclectic mix of Swedish and French furniture. The kitchen splashback wall is lined with traditional glazed green-and-white tiles, while a hefty butcher's block makes a practical work surface. Printed cottons and closely grouped paintings all add to the Gallic country-house atmosphere.

36 Modern Mallorca

Although Mallorca has become an increasingly busy tourist destination and favoured location for holiday homes, it takes only a step back from the coastline to realize that the island still has numerous old farmhouses for sale and some very special sites on which to build. A couple who once bought and restored a house here, originally as a holiday home, quickly made it their permanent base, and developed a thriving building, restoration and design business, catering to busy Europeans who need a reliable and knowledgeable team to create their own dream homes. The owner of this house was a client of theirs who favoured a new house in the country with plenty of shady seating areas, a pool and good-sized casual entertaining spaces, but the open site required a great deal of landscaping before building could begin. Architectural salvage and recycled materials play an important part in the team's designs, providing new houses with a feeling of age and atmosphere. Furniture and fittings are from a wide range of sources, chosen for comfort or patina, shape or suitability. Both architect and designer have created a superb house with more than a nod to the vernacular, and it looks absolutely right in its dramatic island setting.

37 Keeper's cottage

When a London-based American couple chanced on a Victorian cottage on a piece of land deep in the English countryside, the property had little to recommend it apart from a very private location. It did not even have a proper garden. However, the wife, an interior and garden designer, quickly realized that, though small, the house could easily be augmented and, crucially, an old garage could be converted into a guest lodge. She devised a plan to extend the cottage to create a kitchen and dining area with a master bedroom above it. Early on she designed and planted a new garden. More recently, a garden room has been added facing the stream that runs through the plot. The interior spaces have been skilfully reconfigured to create a spacious hall and a new staircase. Pretty oak windows were repaired or replaced, and the old game larder was converted into a cloakroom. The choice of black-painted kitchen units and a black Aga cooker is simple and dramatic. As the cottage is often used as a vacation home in the winter as well as the summer, it is important that the rooms are warm and cosy. The sofas are deep and the bedrooms are decorated in a modern country style, making this renovated cottage a wonderful place for entertaining friends and family.

38 Cornish cream

Located on the Cornish coast in south-west England, close to the sea, this 1960s house was turned into a much-loved family holiday home by the managing director of an international fabrics house. After the doors had been replaced and all reminders of the 1960s removed, it seemed natural to follow the English and American tradition of using tongue-and-groove boarding and stripped and sanded floorboards as a starting point. Although the house is traditional in feel, the use of pale colours, little pattern and functional furniture in simple shapes has established a classic summer look that is airy and light but warm in winter. A deep sofa and comfortable chairs in the main sitting-room are the only really large pieces. An antique chair, painted wooden chairs and cane chairs all look relaxed and casual, and blue has been effectively used, in stripes, checks and solid colour, as an appropriate seaside accent. Naturally the owner loves fabrics, and various linens and cottons have been used throughout the house. Curtains are casually looped up at the corners or left unlined to let in light and fresh air. The stairs have been painted in two tones to imitate a carpet runner, but bare boards are the norm. Relaxed and friendly, this is an ideal holiday home.

39 Summer house

Creamy stone floors, pure-white or off-white walls and natural canvas or linen upholstery and curtains have become the most popular style of decoration in Provence. Not so long ago, it was a different story: a rich red ochre was typically used to colour the walls, the woodwork and often the stone fireplaces; floor-tiles were usually terracotta or coloured geometric designs; fabrics were a riot of colourful, hand-blocked Indiennes prints, most famously produced by the firm of Souleiado in Tarascon. The widespread shift to pale, neutral interiors began in the late 1980s and shows no sign of being over. After completing the restoration of this old stone summer house near Uzès, the London-based owner deliberately kept to a palette of white and the myriad tones of natural wood. On the ground floor the heavy ceiling beams were cleaned but not painted. The only colour used is in the kitchen, where the cupboards and old doors have been treated to a soft green–blue tint, the same colour as that often used – as here – for the exterior shutters. Some of the furniture is painted white, and some elements are old, others new; it is hard to tell the difference. In the intense heat of the Provençal summer this house is a cool and completely relaxing place to be.

40 Traditional manner

A designer and painter chose Northern Cyprus as the ideal location
for his holiday home. Formerly the old village coffee-house, this is a
handsome building, brought back to life and once again in harmony
with the island landscape. Rather than tackle the restoration all at once,
it is an evolving process, the allotted annual works undertaken by local
people and in the traditional manner, but it is no casual holiday project.
Everything is carefully planned and drawn up to guide the workmen.
The paints are natural, locally available pigments, which are light and
vibrant and typical of the Mediterranean, and the original concrete floors
have been coloured with diluted oil paint and given a wax polish. It is
the sort of house that can absorb an exotic mix of items from numerous
countries, such as Uzbekistan, India and Egypt, fusing colour and
texture; things bought purely for pleasure, over many years, look right
here. The East is close at hand, and the garden and exterior living
spaces reflect that influence. The sound of water trickling into pools
creates a wonderfully calm atmosphere, and there are numerous sunny
or shady areas in which to relax.

41 White light

One of the challenges of taking on an unmodernized house is deciding how far to go in terms of restoration and refurbishment. This house in Sussex, built in the 1790s, was a sorry sight on first viewing, but the prospective buyer felt that it had enormous potential and went ahead with the purchase. Multiple layers of paint and varnish were slowly scraped back, revealing a great deal of original panelling, including cupboard doors, but the chimney pieces had been removed and the interior was extremely dark. In addition, the house had no heating and only rudimentary plumbing. The old-fashioned kitchen, with its Belfast sink and wooden worktops, was greatly improved by the addition of a pair of windows either side of the fireplace and by removing old ceiling boards. Tongue-and-groove wall panels and floors lend great charm and a sense of authenticity to an interior; in this case, they have been painted matt white, with the result that the space appears not only larger but also, critically, much lighter. Furnished with a mixture of antiques and junk-shop finds, old Irish linen, white china and stripped pine, the house feels light and airy but has not lost its unique character.

42 Chartreuse charm

Unusually, the garden of this fine and much-loved seventeenth- and eighteenth-century hunting lodge in Périgord, south-west France, was laid out and replanted before the old internal partitions were stripped out to reveal the bones of the house. Unlike the garden, which is filled with roses and lush herbaceous planting, the house has a sparseness that its owner attributes, in part at least, to five years spent living in Japan. The walls are mostly a soft yellow, the floors are bare poplar boards, tiles or stone flags, and there are no curtains and few paintings. The walls are hung instead with groups of prints and drawings, some by Chardin and Henry Moore. Internal shutters control light, and even on a dull day the house glows with a gentle warmth. In the grand salon a pair of bookcases stand either side of the chimney piece, and a Regency panel above it displays prints. Much of the French furniture is painted, and in the petit salon, red fabric from Mali covers the sofa, while two Louis XVI chairs are in a fabric by Le Manach. English rush matting covers the floor. The bathrooms feature old-fashioned claw-foot baths and Pierre Frey fabric lining the cupboards. The chestnut-beamed tower room, formerly a tobacco-drying barn, was opened up for use as a bedroom.

43 Cottage comfort

Many people who change their place of residence from the city to the country are in pursuit of a romantic dream, believing that they will find a better quality of life away from the urban jungle. Others move for professional reasons, to be in a more convenient or more congenial location – as was the case with the owners of this charming cottage. She is a design director for a large fabric house based outside London, and he is a photographer. They wanted a property in the most rural position possible and, when they found this house, decided that they were prepared to endure the three years of work that the project would require. With its low ceilings and colours ranging from pea green to lilac, and from terracotta to clotted cream, the cottage is characterized by rooms that exude warmth and a comfortable intimacy. Old floorboards are softened with colourful rugs or sisal matting, and a pale limestone floor has been laid in the kitchen. In some rooms, woollen blankets are used for curtains, with poles consisting of simple lengths of hazel. Furniture is mismatched in time-honoured country style, fresh flowers abound, and every surface is treated to collections and arrangements of jugs, hats, textiles or quirky objects prized for their shape or colour.

44 Perfect Provence

For many Parisians and an international band of Francophiles, the Lubéron and the area around Saint-Rémy-de-Provence are among the most coveted places in France in which to own a house. Apart from the climate, the views and the wonderful food and wine, there are first-class restorers, designers and craftspeople who can completely transform old farmhouses and manors to suit discriminating owners. This house is a superb example of a major architectural and design collaboration. Virtually everything was replaced, but with great sensitivity to proportion and period detail, and extensive use has been made of reclaimed materials – from floor-tiles and chimney pieces to beams and doors. New stonework was supplied from quarries that have been in use for millennia. The interior decoration was carried out by a friend of the owners who owns a wonderful house near by, is well versed in French style and knows the best sources for fabrics and furniture. Relying largely on white, cream and pale grey, she has created a cool and utterly restful interior of great comfort and style.

45 Country squire

Built in 1580 and fashionably updated in the eighteenth century, this mellow red-brick house in Suffolk is set in 28 hectares (70 acres) of parkland and gardens. Owned by a man who describes himself as a collector, dealer and designer, it has been restored with great care and patience. The stone-flagged entrance hall – a majestic space containing antique busts and an unusual oval marble-column table – sets the scene for a grandly furnished house that is nevertheless warm and welcoming. An inlaid opium bed has been adapted to create an impressive coffee table in the drawing-room, while a pair of overscaled plum-velvet sofas brings to the room a sense of English country-house comfort. Late Victorian baths have been re-enamelled but otherwise left untouched. A reclaimed-slate floor has been installed in the kitchen, and a magnificent handmade copper extractor hood stretches along the wall above the Aga cooker and cabinets. To make the most of the lightness of the interior, the colour scheme has been restricted to a palette of off-whites; the location is so private that window treatments are minimal. One of the twelve bedrooms is furnished with a bed made from very old panels and French barley-twist posts, creating a room evocative of the early nineteenth century, although every room in this elegant house continues to evolve.

46 Forest view

Perched on the very edge of an ancient village surrounded by forest in Lubéron, Provence, this tiny 1650s property is not strictly a country house, but in its interior the owner, a young Frenchman, has used country style mixed with a few quirky modern pieces to great effect. Structurally, the house is almost a column. At ground level, an earth-floored stable has been transformed into an office-cum-workroom. A steep flight of stone steps leads off a tiny, shady courtyard to a floor configured as a bedroom, a bathroom and a winter living-room, which contains a pair of 'zebra' chairs and a colourful rug bought in Paris. The next level faces on to a tiny medieval lane, allowing light into a second living-room; the kitchen beyond is reached through an open arch and furnished with locally made pieces. Unable to use a conventional window, the owner inserted a sheet of glass at ceiling height. To gain extra space, he built a narrow mezzanine above the living-room, a useful area for housing books, a small study table and an unusual chest, each tiny drawer of which is painted a different colour. Right at the top is a terrace from which to enjoy the marvellous views over old tiled roofs and the blue–green forest beyond.

47 Dowager duchess

This old stone dower house in north-east England was in urgent need of sympathy and restoration when the current owners came across it. Originally Elizabethan, it was rebuilt in 1801, but much of its character had been lost after generations of remodelling and partitioning. To create the perfect family home takes courage, talent and the acceptance that so much of the expenditure will be unseen – hidden in walls and roof-space and under floors, as the massive job of installing new plumbing and cabling is carried out. The owner–designer had done it all before, and fortunately all the furniture from the old house fitted perfectly. The ground-floor kitchen and dining-room had been a separate apartment, and once the apartment had been gutted, the owner went to Chalon in London for a new country-style kitchen to complement the large Aga cooker. The first-floor bedrooms and bathrooms are pale but warm. The expansive living areas on the ground floor are richer in detail and colour than those above, employing silks and suede, needlepoint and linen. The design is a triumph of function and country-house comfort.

48 Island refuge

The vernacular architecture of Mallorca is characterized by thick rubble-stone walls, small wood-framed windows and plenty of shady, covered seating and dining areas – features that help explain the island's huge appeal to second-home owners. The climate is good, and until recently there were plenty of old farmhouses there that were ripe for restoration by northern Europeans seeking a place in the sun. A German couple who run an interior-design business knew Mallorca well and decided to acquire a property on the island and create their perfect holiday refuge. The 200-year-old house they bought has been decorated and furnished in a more sophisticated style than would be typical of a simple farmstead, although many local details have been included. The stained-timber kitchen with its open shelving, stone worktops and clay pots is suitably rustic. Bedrooms are light and airy, and the shiny tiled floors are softened by cotton dhurries. In the dining-room a wonderful crystal chandelier has been hung low over the table, and one wall has been covered by a panel painted with a naïve scene. The loggia is furnished for dining with a pair of old painted console tables, an iron daybed and a summery table and chairs; an exotic painted panel links all the colours most effectively.

49 Gothic grace

Located in Sussex, south-east England, and dating from 1820, this unusual stone house was originally a church schoolhouse; it is built in the shape of a cross and has wonderful pointed-arch windows. The owner, a well-known English jewellery designer, realized she had found a gem of a house, and after undertaking major remedial work she began the interior decoration on a room-by-room basis. She enlisted the help of the eminent *trompe l'œil* and paint specialist Graham Carr, who glazed walls and painted cornices and a frieze as well as some of the floors. Carr also designed the bookcases, a chest and a blue-and-white console in the sitting-room, as well as the superb four-poster bed, which is based on a sixteenth-century design. Unusual large mirrors add glamour to the gracious rooms and reflect light from the tall windows. In true country-house tradition, there is an eclectic mix of paintings, sculpture and china. A large African pot has been converted to make a lamp base, for example. Objects have been collected from all over the world, rather in the manner of a mini Grand Tour. Decoration of this style and quality is absolutely timeless and quite beyond fashion.

5o Shared passion

Long-established villages in rural France have a charm all their own. Part of the attraction of such settlements lies in the fact that so many of the old houses remain unrestored, allowing new owners – in this case, a Danish designer of film sets and interiors and his Scottish wife, also an interior designer – to realize their own vision of a perfect home. Close to the vineyards and chateaux of Bordeaux, this classic house, built between 1640 and the mid-nineteenth century, has two distinct faces. The front overlooks the market square, while the rear has glorious, uninterrupted views of the countryside. Many of the original elements – fireplaces, shutters, floors and panelling – have been preserved and renovated. The generous proportions of the building give enough space for four large bedrooms and four bathrooms. White paint throughout, together with the many metres of John England Irish linen used for curtains and upholstery, creates a light and soothing background for an eclectic mix of furniture, ranging from antiques and old pictures to pieces from Ikea. A wonderfully original idea is the decorative use of numerous wine boxes, with their labels attached, to line the kitchen walls. The large scale of the dark metal lanterns and chandeliers works particularly well against the high, white ceilings.

51 Crown jewel

-An ancient house with royal connections and its own land has for centuries been at the centre of a certain kind of English aspiration. Such properties have often been much reduced in size or conversely, in the case of smaller houses, added to over the centuries, and present owners have to make numerous tough decisions about their future. This house bankrupted its builder in the sixteenth century, and later much of the enormous building was demolished. Even so, a sizeable portion remained, which was again extended in the 1800s. The house has been owned by the same family ever since. The current occupants recognize and enjoy the ups and downs of living in a historic property, including the fact that today such a house and garden have to pay their own way. Restoration is a constant consideration, with much of the investment going unseen into roof repairs or renewing electrical systems, but a great deal of the extraordinary charm of old houses lies in the many surviving layers of previous generations' pictures, furniture and fabrics. Bathrooms and kitchens have been updated but in an old-fashioned style and, while the house is a busy family home, there is a palpable sense of history in every room. It takes great skill and energy to keep such a house so fresh and alive.

5² Understated elegance

Not long ago, this former farmhouse in Provence was no more than a rundown stone cottage with several small agricultural sheds attached, all standing on a 1.6-hectare (4-acre) site. Luckily, the next-door neighbour became interested in the property and asked some friends of his, restorers and designers based in Aix-en-Provence, to draw up plans to redevelop it as a guest house. The project went ahead, and the original property is now unrecognizable. Complying with the strict local planning regulations, the restoration experts have created a dream home. Specialists in regional architecture and pioneers of a new Provençal interior style, they have used fine polished stone and natural oak boards for the floors and kept the plastered walls plain white. Red is the accent colour inside and out. Simple printed and striped cottons characterize most rooms, but a grander gesture has been made in the main living-room, in the design of a large, armless, back-to-back sofa upholstered in a woven fabric with an overscaled pattern. Moroccan reed mats soften the floors, and unlined fine-linen curtains shade the bedrooms. Iron tables and lamps, African pieces and the beautifully crafted bathrooms and kitchen add to the sense of understated luxury.

53 Country classic

The English country house was, and still is, an important inspiration for many international designers, but there is nothing quite like the real thing. Formed of a central block built in 1680 and an extension of identical wings on either side, dating from 1720, this ochre-washed brick house has barely changed since it was completed. Minor alterations were made to the interiors in the late twentieth century: the kitchen floor was raised, a warren of service rooms behind the rear staircase was opened up to become an informal sitting-room, and glass doors were added to the dining-room, giving access to a garden terrace. Several bedrooms became bathrooms, fitted out in period style with deep free-standing baths and plenty of large cupboards. The old wide-plank floors and staircases are original, and the decoration is pure country classic, relying on collections of textiles, antique furniture, mirrors, porcelain and faded oriental rugs, and creating the impression of generations of occupation by the same family. The walls and panelling are painted in off-whites to balance the patterns, colours and textures of contemporary and antique textiles used for curtains and upholstery.

54 Hidden gem

Set 200 metres (655 ft) above a valley of farmland near Ménerbes in the South of France is a house that has been created from a very old farm, at its heart a vaulted stone *bergerie* in which livestock were originally housed. Although magnificent gardens have been planted, the property also incorporates wild areas of forest and ancient trackways that were used for centuries to link the hilltop villages of the area. The owners, who live here year-round, took advice on colours, furniture and fabrics from a well-known interior designer and decorator based in Aix-en-Provence. The long, hot summers are conducive to outdoor living, with the property incorporating expansive outside living areas and a vast swimming pool. In contrast, the inside of the house is decorated in warm colours, with oriental rugs and vibrant traditional fabrics: schemes that provide a cosy environment in winter. A fine collection of furniture, some of it eighteenth century, together with top-quality pictures and numerous books, creates a certain air of grandeur that would no doubt amaze the farmer who lived here years ago.

55 Coastal heritage

Everything about the interior of this house suits its remarkable location on England's Dorset coast, an area that was declared a World Heritage Site in 2002. The house, one of a pair, was built in the 1880s as a holiday home. The current owner, a designer, had dreamed of a seaside home for years and had rented cottages near by for some time, but never expected she would find the right house as easily as she did. The property had been a guest house for many years, and a formidable amount of work was required to upgrade the entire building. The former double garage became a very large kitchen/dining-room, designed to have the best possible views of the sea. The front-facing wall is entirely glass; the owner enclosed the large terrace across the façade but allowed for plenty of windows, one of which is framed by a weathered teak door frame. All the paintwork was bought or mixed to echo the colours of the local cliffs and fossils, and old pallets, driftwood and scaffolding have become shelves and cupboards. Although the scene is undoubtedly English, this interesting house has a colonial ambience about it that is relaxed, airy and supremely comfortable.

56 Reinventing the past

Set above a stretch of coastline in southern France, this eighteenth-century house has been treated to a highly sensitive, almost invisible restoration, which began with the demolition of nineteenth-century additions to reveal the original structure. Its owner, an interior architect and designer, has a passion for peeling paint, original finishes and period fittings. He added windows for extra light and set about revealing the age-old wall colours, floor-tiles, doors and shutters. He essentially turned the house upside-down. The ground floor now consists of an entrance hall and a spare room. The first floor comprises a bedroom, a bathroom and a landing used as a library; while the top floor, formerly a series of tiny rooms, has been opened up to create the living, dining and kitchen areas. Local antiques shops and *brocantes* provided most of the antique furniture, along with rustic garden chairs, old 'foxed' mirrors and lighting. The only modern piece is a comfortable sofa covered in old linen sheets. Apart from a touch of blue–green in the kitchen and a red-and-white-striped cushion, there is little colour in the house; decorative interest comes from the textures and natural tones of wood, plaster and metal.

57 Anglo-American

Warm climates demand architecture that allows a house and garden to be far more accessible to each other than is common in northern Europe. Open verandas, perhaps slatted shutters to admit fresh air, and plenty of glazed doors are the norm, allowing the house to be opened up from back to front in the hot summer months. The interiors, however, can range from seaside resort to cosy country, and here an English owner asked a local designer to interpret an Anglo-American approach to a new house, set in idyllic surroundings on a lake in Georgia. It is a rich mix of antique, reproduction and contemporary furniture, textured fabrics, patterns and colour. Some corners of the house are definitely English in style; there is French country as well as American Federal furniture; and there are pieces of oriental blue-and-white porcelain. Chairs and tables are set out on the wraparound verandas, with the walls lined in white-painted clapboard. Tall trees set in trim green lawns shade parts of the house, and the views over the water are sensational.

58 Mill house

Built in the mid-eighteenth century, this former flour-mill in Hampshire, England, was converted to residential use in the 1930s by an architect who was strongly influenced by the Arts and Crafts movement. Many of the handcrafted timber elements have survived and been enhanced by the current owners. After converting outbuildings to give themselves extra space, the couple, who are both designers, removed unwanted ceiling boards and partitions to expose supporting oak beams, thereby highlighting the building's rustic construction. Rather than imitating a country-cottage style or trying to create a coordinated interior, they chose furnishings that they love. Some pieces were inherited; others were designed and made by one of the owners. A pair of large Knoll sofas was bought specially for the house, and artistic friends and local craftspeople created many of the pictures and ceramics. Colour was an important factor, since the abundance of wood in floors, ceiling beams and staircase could have felt overwhelming. The new white table and chairs look stylish under the timber-and-glass roof. House conversions may sometimes seem disjointed, but this harmonious example carries echoes of the building's working past while providing for modern living.

59 La bergerie

Thought to have been built in the 1520s, the magnificent living-room of this western Provençal house was a *bergerie* (sheepfold) – but one of some architectural merit, and filled one side of a courtyard. There is little evidence from the outside of what is to be found within: a great room of white stone floors and white walls divided by elegant stone arches and furnished with a fascinating collection of furniture and objects from ancient to modern. In so large a space the scale of the furniture needs to be carefully considered, and items should be grouped in different parts of the room with open areas between. Particularly interesting is a disparate group of chairs set around a table covered with books, an irresistible place to mull over art or architectural tomes. The central portion of the white-shuttered house contains the owner's private quarters, while opposite is an area for guests, with a bedroom exuberantly decorated in red-and-white fabric. Above a studio area a flight of steps leads to a small covered terrace somewhat reminiscent of Tuscan style. The courtyard is a triumph of design and planting, offering strong shape, colour and scent and providing a link to expansive new gardens beyond, inspired by the sixteenth-century Ottoman architect Sinan.

6o Country comfort

Although varied in terms of architecture and size, English country houses are generally associated with expectations of warmth, comfort, informality and pleasure. The smaller examples of the style, especially if they are typically Georgian in design, have become increasingly popular and expensive, and few have survived unaltered. Built not by the aristocracy but perhaps by members of the clergy, successful farmers or tradesmen, they work as well today, in terms of proportion, light and layout, as they did when they were constructed. The London-based couple who own this mid-seventeenth-century house in the West Country were not concerned that changes had been made to the property, first in the eighteenth century and again in 1820. They decided that, apart from renewing the roof and windows, they would subject the house to a sensitive and minimal refurbishment. For example, unless disfigured by flaking paint, the walls were left undisturbed. Wallpaper was preserved or copied, existing paint colours were matched and fabrics were chosen to suit the owners' collection of antique furniture. Even the bathrooms, which are new, are pleasingly old-fashioned in style.

61 Entente cordiale

The owners of this estate near Le Mans in France have combined their possessions and style with great accord. The wife, an English interior designer, and her French husband took on the 1806 Directoire property immediately after their marriage. A pretty two-storey house with numerous guest bedrooms, some of which are set behind dormer windows in the roof, it has the classic, highly desirable proportions of the period. A broad, raised stone terrace graces the front, while in the centre is a double entrance hall, the staircase rising from a smaller hall behind. To the left is a large reception room, and beyond it another, used for shooting parties, runs the full depth of the house. Reached by way of a bright corridor is the dining-room, and beyond that a large library, which links to the kitchen. The decoration throughout relies on a mix of wonderful antique furniture and English and French textiles. There is an old walled farmyard behind the house, and ponds, woods and fields surround the property, creating a private haven of peace and quiet.

6 2 Gothic folly

The English fashion in the eighteenth and early nineteenth centuries for building parkland follies has led to some intriguing twentieth-century conversions. Designed as hunting lodges, bath-houses or picnic pavilions, follies were frequently set in sublime landscapes. This Gothic example was rebuilt and restored as a weekend retreat by a London-based dealer in Old Masters and his friend, an interior designer. By using salvaged materials, moving the staircase, replacing the doors and windows and changing the floor levels, the owners achieved a more practical use of the space. The paint colours on the walls – warm yellows, buff and red – set off a collection of blue-and-white Chinese plates and lamps. The furniture and pictures, a mixture of equestrian subjects, botanical studies and landscapes, were chosen to complement the architecture. Chippendale-style chairs flanking an octagonal dining table, gilt-framed mirrors, small chests and a writing desk all look perfectly at home in the space. The bedrooms are curtained with archive-print fabrics simply hung from poles. As there are no neighbours, many of the windows have been left bare, affording the expansive views that are one of the main attractions of a folly.

6₃ Traditional spirit

There are numerous difficult decisions to make during the restoration of an old house. Achieving balance between retaining the character and patina of age, while bringing services and the flow of space up to date, can be a daunting task, and the owners of this Mallorcan house called in a respected designer to pull the project together. The house was a ruin but, by taking great care to use local materials and finishes, they have created a home of great charm that is suitable for both a modern lifestyle and the sunny island setting. Floor finishes vary widely, from terracotta to pebble and tile. The interiors are relaxed, light and airy, using shades of white, cream and soft blue and green; beams are bleached or left in their natural wood tones. The furniture, most of which is antique European, is either painted or waxed wood, and the choice of fabrics is summery and pale. Taking the view that they wanted neither a town nor a country look, the owners have mixed up the contents in a relaxed manner, enlivening the pale scheme with touches of vivid red, blue or black.

64 Eastern influence

It is not surprising that Provençal houses feature widely in this book. Large or small, usually built of light-coloured local stone and set in lovely surroundings, they are mostly rural dwellings that evolved over time as farmers' needs dictated, and have proved ideal subjects for restoration. Tucked up against rocky outcrops and ancient terracing, and sheltered by towering pine trees, this house is a classic example of the evolution of one such country house. The depth of the house was determined by the length of available structural tree-trunk beams; the only two-storeyed section, now converted into bedrooms and bathrooms, would originally have been used for agricultural storage. Owned by an English couple who spent many years in the Far East, the house is furnished with a delightful mix of Asian textiles from Laos, Myanmar (Burma), China and Hong Kong, all of which add colour and texture to the simple stone or white-painted walls. The walls forming the sheltered rear courtyard, not visible from the front, have been painted cerulean, an intense colour that works well in the glittering light of the region. While the house is traditional vernacular, the choice of colourful, exotic textiles and blue-and-white china imparts a relaxed and elegant feel.

65 Material benefits

Appearances can be deceptive. This English house was built in the 1950s in the style of the early twentieth century. The current owner, an artist and garden designer, saw through the building's years of neglect and its lack of interesting architectural detail to realize that it offered huge scope for improvement. Some surviving oak detailing on the exterior, coupled with the owner's love of barns, inspired a major refurbishment, which centred on the construction of a two-bay, two-storey oak-framed extension and dining conservatory designed by the owner herself. The use of green oak for the construction and red bricks and Chinese slate for the floors has created a sense of solidity and permanence. The house is now full of textural interest and, above all, wonderful natural light. As much glass as possible has been used, particularly in the new first-floor bedroom; glass panels were set into the roof, and windows and doors were inserted on three sides of the room, including the fireplace wall. Painted a warm ochre, the living areas appear to be bathed in sunlight. The same colour was used for the retaining walls of the terraced garden, establishing a clever link between the interior and exterior spaces.

66 Fine form

An Anglo-American couple, who collect, restore and deal in antiques, have created a stunning interior in an old house in Arles, south-west France. A sculptural limestone staircase, worn by centuries of use, provides access to a series of levels, each with a definite style. Traditional hexagonal terracotta tiles set the scene in the living-rooms, with the walls washed in a pale yellow, and the ceilings, with their close-set beams, decorated with scroll and leaf patterns. The kitchen is a gloriously old-fashioned creation reminiscent of a still-life oil painting. With such high ceilings, attention to the scale of furniture and objects was important. The master bedroom contains antique Chinese priests' chairs, Japanese Imari-ware and a seventeenth-century Kangxi (Qing dynasty) vase, as well as a Ming dynasty signed bronze gong. The large house is not crowded with furniture; rather, each piece has been carefully chosen because it is a fine example of its type. The furniture is enhanced by a collection of figurines, busts and porcelain. Yet there is a pleasing simplicity to this rather grand house, in part because no curtains or blinds cover the tall windows, the colour schemes are quiet and the restoration was carried out to a very high standard using appropriate materials.

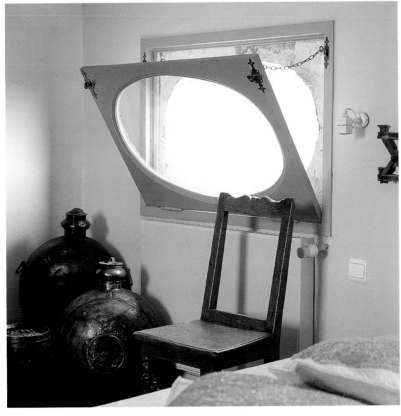

67 Defying fashion

When this old family home in England passed to a younger generation, it was inevitable that changes would be made. The house, built in about 1820, was taken in hand by a woman who not only is an experienced designer but also deals in antique and twentieth-century furniture. The interior design and decoration were reviewed, and consideration was given to improving the layout and proportions of the rooms. A plan was devised to build a substantial extension to house a new drawing-room on the ground floor, with bedrooms and bathrooms above. Simplifying and opening up the kitchen meant removing an old butler's pantry and a staircase, but the extra space and light have proved a great bonus. New windows were chosen to harmonize with the old and, where possible, reclaimed materials have been used, including flagstones for the linking hall; door handles, taps, basins and radiators are all period pieces. A set of antique doors opens into the drawing-room, and the floorboards were cut from old beams. The owners like understated eighteenth-century Continental furniture, rich detailing and fine fabrics set against soft, organic paintwork; tall gilt mirrors make a strong vertical statement. This house displays confident English design at its very best.

68 Highland fling

Very few people actually buy castles, but this magnificent sixteenth-century colossus on the edge of the Firth of Moray in Scotland was found and restored by a man who, since childhood, had dreamed of owning and restoring such a place. Although bought as a ruin, it was nonetheless a late medieval Z-plan tower. Armed with little money but plenty of knowledge and lots of enthusiasm, the owners embarked on a seven-year restoration programme. It was a labour of love: eighty-six windows and doors were made by local craftspeople; the correct timber, slate and stone had to be found; and, keen to avoid using any wrong materials, the owners mixed the lime and pigments for the exterior finish themselves. Fortunately, their textile and carpet business manufactures designs with a Scottish history and palette, and they were able to use a great many of their own products throughout the interior. Some of the furniture was made at the castle and other pieces were inherited or bought locally. The walls are clad with either wooden planks or softly painted plaster, the windows are curtainless, but the beds and sofas are draped and warmed with hangings, blankets and woollen fabrics. An enormous challenge, this is a dream come true.

69 Rural refinement

The 'before' photographs of this magnificent bastide outside Aix-en-Provence beggar belief. There was a house on the site, but such was the vision of the owners and the architectural studio they employed to create their dream home that there is now no sign of what existed before. The result is a supremely elegant eighteenth-century-style marvel set amid gardens and parkland on rising ground and with unparalleled views, and it has become the frequently visited holiday home of a London-based couple and their children. The house is perfectly proportioned and laid out. To the right of the stone-flagged entrance hall are the dining-room and the large contemporary kitchen. To the left are the living-rooms, each of which has tall doors opening on to terraces. The interiors are a harmonious mix of soft colours, ranging from stone and grey to buff and ivory. Unusual antiques are combined with modern pieces, and in every room there is a considered blend of texture, colour and pattern. This is a country house that has been designed for all seasons using the finest quality materials both inside and out; classic but contemporary in every respect, it is a house that appeals to all the senses.

70 Peak practice

Everything about this highly individual and unusual home and business is a surprise. It is in the Peak District National Park, near the English city of Sheffield, and has been created from a group of old industrial buildings that have been converted to include a manufacturing enterprise, a shop, a home and a studio. The live/work ethic has always appealed to some people, and here a former gas plant and ancillary buildings have been turned into a glorious property through the vision of the owner and the architect. Two rectangular stone buildings are linked at first-floor level. One, the owner's home, contains bedrooms and bathrooms at ground level and an open-plan kitchen, dining and living area lit from above by glass sections set into the timber-lined roof. The adjacent building houses a studio on the first floor, which is furnished with Eames and Alvar Aalto chairs and an Arts and Crafts sideboard. There is also an extensive collection of books, which are wonderfully accessible in library-style open shelving units. Below the cavernous studio is the shop, and beside this group of buildings is an award-winning round stone structure where the design and manufacture of cutlery takes place. To live and work within a national park is a rare treat.

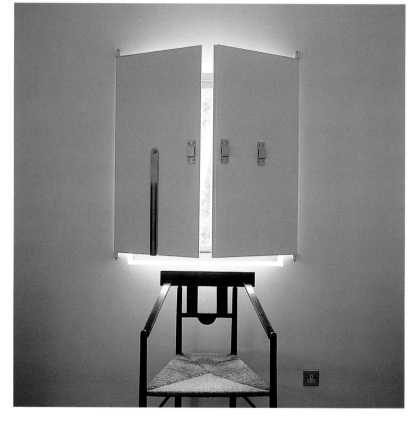

71 Rooms with a view

An ideal location for a country house is one that provides good views, and this Provençal house enjoys an exceptional panorama of farms, fields and mountains spreading out on three sides; a fascinating medieval castle and village tower above it all. Work had been carried out on the house in the 1960s, but when new owners arrived they had more sympathetic ideas for its restoration and, in particular, for the creation of a garden. Not everything in the house is strictly French, there being a mix of locally bought and English pieces, yet the interiors have a particularly French feel. Architecturally, of course, the heavily beamed ceilings and creamy stone floors are unmistakably local, while a zinc-topped unit in the kitchen came from a local café, and the rosewood guest bed is typical of nineteenth-century French taste. A number of pieces of brown furniture have been painted white, giving them a new lease of life, and in the case of old chairs re-upholstered in natural linen, a surprisingly modern air. Various Moroccan straw mats in traditional cream and red are a perfect choice for country stone floors such as these.

72 Natural conclusion

The wooded rocky landscape of south-east Mallorca was the natural choice for a sculptor wanting to build a new house on the island. She was determined not to destroy the site in any way, and planned the design and construction in order to maximize the use of contemporary green technologies. The conservation of water was a particularly important aspect of the design. Part of the building already existed (a house built about seventy years ago), to which was added an adjoining structure built of the local stone, steel and glass. All the floors are polished stone; some of the internal walls were left in their rough stone state, while others were rendered with a mix of finely ground stone and cement. No paint was used, the pale colour throughout gained from the natural materials. Apart from an old English lounger, most of the furniture was bought on the island: simple white cotton-covered sofas and cane chairs and a pure-white marble dining table. The timber ceiling beams are original to the old house, and all the doors and windows have wooden frames, but the new wing, housing the bedrooms and bathrooms, features frameless openings. The owner, who works in steel, lead, wood and stone, has created an admirable year-round dwelling completely at one with the land.

73 Treetop retreat

Living in a tree house might not be everyone's idea of bliss, but in the case of this owner it was a dream that began in childhood and has persisted all his life. A suitable, large pine tree was found in the grounds of his home in Provence, and discussions with a friend led to the drawing up of numerous designs for a variety of fantastic tree houses. It was a technically challenging task to build a sufficiently light structure on a support that would not damage the host tree. In the event, an ingenious rubber-lined steel girth was devised to allow the slow expansion of the tree trunk over time. The house itself is reminiscent of a tiny colonial cottage constructed entirely from cedar. Glass-less windows are made of wood, and a small hole has been cut in the centre of each to allow air to circulate when the window is closed. Simple folding chairs and a timber bench provide seating, and a console table is fixed to one wall. There is an outdoor deck on which to sit while contemplating the landscape or anything else one might want to consider in this most private and captivating of retreats.

74 Country continuity

With a house built in the seventeenth and eighteenth centuries, a horse stud and 810 hectares (2000 acres) of land, an English country estate such as this is one of the most prized pieces of property in the world. The well-proportioned rooms, wonderful windows, ancient floorboards and nooks and crannies that lend themselves to many different uses are the stuff of dreams. Unusually, all the windows in the house have been left free of curtains. Preferring natural illumination both during the day and at night, the owners have decided that shutters and white roller blinds are all that are necessary. Also unusual is the fact that the interior is painted in a range of different whites, from lime-white and gardenia to a pale mushroom. There are few sources of colour, apart from several rugs, the collection of oil paintings and jugs of fresh flowers. Waxed pine, polished mahogany and the varying colours of the wooden floors create a gentle continuity throughout the house, replacing rooms themed by colour, wallpaper or fabric. It is a modern look for a very old house, and an approach that has become extremely popular.

75 Expert restoration

The weathered and ancient front door provides no clue as to what one might find on entering this Provençal house, but immediately an enchanting hall promises surprises. Dimly lit and full of atmosphere, the hall leads to a stone staircase that draws one up to a magnificent enclosed courtyard garden, two sides of which are formed by the house itself. The adjacent wall is certainly thirteenth-century, and the house is known to have been a stopping-place for members of the Church travelling from Rome to Avignon to visit the pope. The poet, scientist and doctor Nostradamus was born near by. The present owners, who are Dutch, called in an expert and highly respected local architectural practice to carry out a complete renovation and redesign. Masters of the Provençal vernacular, the team has built a most elegant home from somewhat inauspicious beginnings. The mainly French and English furnishings and fabrics were chosen by the owners to complement the typically eighteenth-century-French greys and muted pastels of the flat paintwork – a timeless combination.

76 Magic Mallorca

A rural residence, especially in a country with a warm climate, can never be entirely divorced from its surrounding land or gardens. This is particularly true in Mallorca, where the old stone fincas (farmhouses) appear to have grown organically from the bedrock. Covered terraces are important living spaces; in this case, a series of broad stone arches creates the sense of an indoor room, but the space is breezy and full of light. Comfortable seating is provided in the shape of relaxed and manoeuvrable cane chairs. Chunky, close-set structural timber beams are the dominant feature in most of the rooms in the finca. Some people in Mallorca choose to treat their interiors in a strictly modern manner; others take a relaxed country approach to furnishing and decorating, mixing local antiques with French, English or Scandinavian furniture. Having established an interior-design and furnishing shop on the island, the owners had accumulated a great deal of knowledge about vernacular building styles, which they have successfully incorporated into their own home. With their pale sandstone floors and whitewashed walls, the rooms have been treated to a palette of natural colours, neutral linens, cotton tickings and the occasional print.

77 Home and away

Living in Hong Kong but planning in the long term to return to England when their children reached school age, a couple enlisted the help of the wife's father, a recently retired architect, to find a perfect family home. The brief stipulated that it had to have easy access to London, a great view and plenty of space and light – a tall order, but one that produced an admirable result. Prepared to undertake extensive work, they found a country house in a perfect location down a quiet lane in Surrey. The architect and his daughter, a designer, set about the plans, largely by fax and telephone. The rather uninspiring farmhouse was turned into an enviably large, light home with an elegant façade, which included the construction of a double-height Regency-style curved front. Old barns were demolished to create a vast kitchen and informal dining area, beyond which are a family sitting-room, the designer's office and garages. There is a lightness of touch about the interiors that reminds one of colonial living – few curtains, cotton slip-covered furniture, Asian antiques and coir matting on bare floorboards. The bedrooms are pale but cosy, with marble bathrooms.

78 Perennial favourite

Records indicate that parts of this house in eastern Provence are around 900 years old. Its English owners are well-known local antiques dealers; specializing in seventeenth- and eighteenth-century French, Italian and Scandinavian furniture, they were thus well placed to decorate and furnish the house in the most appropriate and stylish manner, having once restored it. The house is set over four floors, the lowest level being a stone-lined, cavelike space where some kind of artisan business would originally have been conducted. The painted country-style kitchen-cum-dining-room and a large living-room, both of which have yellow-ochre-washed walls, take up the ground floor. Blue woad-dyed linen bought in France has been used for some of the curtains and cushions, while natural ecru linen was chosen for sofas and chairs in a variety of styles and shapes. The bedrooms are light, summery and prettily decorated in a classic theme of blue and white, using checks, toile, voile and traditional cotton quilts, and featuring some fine antique painted furniture. This is a perennially popular style of relaxed decoration where old and new are mixed but nothing looks out of place.

79 On Nantucket

A London-based German interior designer and her family spend their
holidays on the island of Nantucket, off the coast of Massachusetts,
in a house that was originally just a tiny two-bedroom cottage. The
designer discovered that it could be enlarged and took on the project
herself, with the help of an architect who, critically, could advise on any
planning restrictions. There are many historic buildings on the island,
and preserving the vernacular style was important. The roof space was
opened up and a large garage converted into a kitchen (with an English
Aga set into a niche) and a spacious dining-room. The attic provided
several bedrooms and bathrooms. As the house is used year-round, the
owner included a fireplace, which has full-height bookshelves on either
side. The interior decoration suits the location, only minutes from the
beach: pine floorboards, white Lloyd Loom furniture and striped cotton-
covered sofas are relaxed and casual, and the tongue-and-groove
boarding suits the mood and the architecture. Mixing contemporary
furniture with several antique pieces gives a holiday home a feeling
of permanence and provides a change of shape and texture against
such a neutral background.

8o Balmy Balearics

Mediterranean country style is exemplified in this relaxed Mallorcan interior, which was restored by two German designers. The surviving rough stone walls and structural timber beams dictated the way in which the owners chose to decorate and furnish the house. The furniture consists of a charming mixture of rustic tables and chairs, comfortable modern sofas, a crystal chandelier and casual striped flat-weave rugs. Traditionally small windows with shutters meant that there was no need for curtains, but plenty of hard-wearing white denim was used for bed curtains and upholstery. Two terraces – one at ground level, the other on the roof – are treated as outdoor living- and dining-rooms and have been adorned with locally made pots and Mediterranean plants. Wherever possible, the owners have used only local materials and, being designers, have taken great care to respect the vernacular architecture, an attitude that enhances the joy of living in a historic and aesthetically pleasing environment.

81   Georgian tradition

Set on rising ground within park-like gardens, this late Georgian house in mid-Wales was not in good repair when its owners first saw it, but the location, the views and the absence of neighbours convinced them that it could easily become a dream home. Architecture of this period is, of course, much sought-after. Room sizes and their number are usually good, often allowing generous en-suite bathrooms; window proportions have never been bettered; staircases are often top-lit; and, if luck will have it, a number of good marble fireplace surrounds will have survived. The owner of this property is a London art dealer who specializes in British paintings, and his wife is an interior designer, so there was never any doubt that the refurbishment and decoration of their fairly large country house would be anything but a superb example of the genre. Naturally there are many wonderful works of art here, ranging from large equestrian canvases to small portraits. A warren of utility rooms has become an adjoining kitchen and breakfast-room, French in style, with doors leading to the garden. All the bedrooms are furnished in the best country-house traditions of gentle colour, comfort and warmth.

82 Yorkshire manor house

This large house in the North of England was described as a 'blank
canvas' to begin with. Its owners, a couple with three young children,
had a limited budget with which to decorate and furnish completely
their imposing home. Large rooms and high ceilings can be a daunting
prospect, with decorating mistakes being expensive to rectify. Fortunately,
the wife had worked in interior design for a number of years, and she
quickly realized that the entrance hall, with its sweeping staircase with
iron balustrades, was an important starting point and would set the scene
for the rest of the house. The pale, washable, fleur-de-lis wallpaper was
an excellent choice for the hall. Paint is the least expensive way to update
a room, and by picking out architectural details in a contrasting colour
and treating the shutters in the same way, the owners have made the
dining-room a lively, glowing space. Warm colours are often a happy
choice in a northern climate, so for the family sitting-room a strong
ochre-pink wall colour was the starting point, with a cream carpet and
woodwork forming a pleasing contrast. The curvy sofa was covered in
a selection of complementary-coloured remnants collected over the
years. The kitchen is decorated in blue and yellow, a popular choice for
a family kitchen.

8 3 French leave

A charming nineteenth-century house in the Marne valley in France is where a well-known New Zealand artist lives and works, in a setting that is not so very different from her rural homeland. Admittedly, however, nobody in the Antipodes built houses like this – a charming bourgeois brick-and-stone mini chateau with numerous tall timber-framed windows screened by grey–blue painted shutters. Although the house was described as a ruin inside when it was bought, the interiors nonetheless still contained typical terracotta floor-tiles, old exposed beams and some cupboards. Within the restored shell a quirky mix of partitions has been added, designed to fulfil the owner's very specific requirements. Fitted within the formerly empty first floor is a plywood structure that divides the space into a bedroom, a sizeable library, a bathroom and an office. Much creative work has gone into enlivening the tired old rooms: paintings abound, of course, but also collections as unusual as they are decorative. The garden is a constant source of joy and produce, while the house provides an inspirational backdrop to artistic endeavour.

84 English eccentric

For lovers of mid-eighteenth-century English architecture, this Wiltshire property is the dream home. With a walled garden, a coach house and a wild garden large enough to keep chickens, pigs (as the owners do) or perhaps a horse, it is a house that stirs the emotions. The interiors were created largely by the present owner's father, who painted the brown-toned design on to the walls of the first-floor landing and hung original William Morris wallpaper (dating from about 1910) in the small sitting-room. All the furniture, except a Rose Tarlow sofa, is well-worn and chintz-covered or cushioned with antique fabrics, many bought at country-house sales. The table in the hall was made on site by fitting a seventeenth-century oak top on to new legs. The dining-room, formerly the kitchen, retains a massive original fireplace, which would have been used for cooking. Each room has a display of paintings and prints, from Piranesi and Raphael to family portraits and photography by Angus McBean. Spanning the width of the dining-room wall is a framed nineteenth-century Tapa (bark) cloth from the Pacific. This wonderful family home has been created by different generations with no desire to change anything, and in it one is barely aware of the twenty-first century.

85 Var vineyard

A beautiful country house is a splendid thing in itself, but this property in the Var region of France also includes a vineyard of nearly 30 hectares (75 acres); the Canadian owner's son is a winemaker and his wife is skilled at interior decoration in the French style. When the family first arrived, the seventeenth-century property had been abandoned for twenty-five years. During the restoration work, the remains of Roman aqueducts were discovered, reflecting the region's long history of agricultural productivity. The house's magnificent rose-pink façade, comprising four bays, is punctuated by arched French windows leading on to a deep, shady terrace that stretches across the full width of the building. Rationalizing the layout of the rooms took time, with a series of large spaces being created, all of which have been painted white, apart from the winter dining-room with its warm coral tones. The couple had previously lived in several countries and travelled a great deal, so the furniture is a lovely mix of French and English furniture bought in Canada, sofas from Geneva, rugs from India, and bedroom curtains fashioned from old linen bed sheets; the dining-room table was found in Ireland. It is a large house decorated with great panache.

86 Cliff-top retreat

One of the best aspects of a holiday home is the fact that the practical issues of everyday life, such as storage space, are largely irrelevant. Utter simplicity is often the key, especially in a warm climate, where the house is almost secondary to the outside. Set on a cliff-top above the sea in Mallorca, this one-room cottage, which only recently gained a supply of running water, was built by the native owner's grandfather. Apart from improving the plumbing, the grandson has also erected a Moorish-style wall across the width of the cottage to create a sleeping and living area; in one niche is a gas hob, in another a sink, while shelves store basic kitchen equipment. Behind the wall are a tiny shower and WC. The old fireplace, used in the past for cooking and heating, has been retained. Time spent here is mainly on the terraces, which are bedecked with colourful rugs and cushions, and a table with comfortable wicker chairs, to enable the owners to enjoy the views of the sea below.

87 Art house

The artist owner of this eighteenth-century house in eastern England is a committed colourist who believes that white rooms are dull, both to paint in and to live in. Each room in the house may be painted in several tones of one colour, and the hue of the woodwork may differ from that of the walls, but the colours in a single room are always closely related to one another. These gentle, friendly rooms have been furnished with pieces collected over many years: some inherited, others bought at local salerooms. The effect of slowly adding favourite finds – a chair here, a side table there – makes it seem as if the rooms have evolved naturally over several generations. Closely grouped works of art are key to the success of the look. The kitchen is the most authentically rural space in the house, but there are plenty of other country-style elements, including large, comfortable beds, capacious chests of drawers, cosy rugs on the floors and pretty second-hand curtains at the windows. The house is used for a variety of purposes. As well as being a family home, it is both a painter's studio and a place where painting courses are run.

88 Another country

Approached along a narrow country road, with a barren rocky ridge on one side and flat, expansive farmland on the other, this grand bastide sits raised on a broad terrace, seemingly untouched for centuries. All is not what it seems, but so sensitive was the expert restoration of this range of Provençal barns that it is hard to imagine that this house was recently a ruin. The owners are American, the wife an interior designer who might have been an acolyte of Madame de Pompadour, such is her love of eighteenth-century French design and decoration. The architectural firm that carried out the work is renowned for its knowledge of period detail and ability to source the correct materials, be they fireplaces or window glass. While many of the rooms are filled with superb pieces from the period, this is a relaxed family home with numerous guest bedrooms, great entertaining spaces and intimate private quarters. Matt-grey and milky-white paintwork sets off collections of early Gien faience, old oil paintings, Provençal fruitwood furniture and elaborate gilt frames. Many of the contents were bought locally, while fabrics came from Pierre Frey in Paris or from the United States. Highly detailed planning and the expertise of both owner and architect have created an exceptional family home, imbued with history and great presence.

89 Lakeland leisure

The owner of this converted sixteenth-century stone barn in the English Lake District called upon some designer friends to help overhaul the interiors, with the aim of creating a comfortable weekend retreat for year-round use. To make better use of the small space, a wall between the hall and the living-room was removed, but the rest of the layout remained as it was. The starting point was the choice of a wall colour – one that would work for every room, providing continuity and, importantly, increasing the sense of space. Mustard-yellow was an ideal option, warm but light and a good neutral background. Similarly, all the floors are covered with seagrass matting. The old kitchen units were retained and painted the same colour as the walls. Demonstrating that overscaled pieces can work well in small rooms, a four-poster bed almost fills the master bedroom, made cosy with handmade hangings and a printed Indian quilt. A simple country chair, faux bamboo side tables and a pair of seventeenth-century carvings complete the country look. Instead of artworks, an Indian tablecloth fixed to batons fills a wall above the living-room sofa, while a large mirror reflects light and balances the shape of the slate fireplace.

90 Gallic style

Screened by old oak trees and flanked by an orchard of pears, plums and apples, this seventeenth-century former priory in Normandy was restored by its Francophile owner, an interior designer, in the best French tradition. Used as a farmhouse after the Revolution, the house is now reminiscent of a charming miniature eighteenth-century *manoir*. With little structural restoration required, it was a matter of transforming interiors decorated in a dull 1960s style into a restrained and elegant modern home. Hessian was stripped off the walls; the old brickwork was exposed in the dining-room and living-room; and all the flush doors were replaced with period panelled ones. Dados and Louis XIII mouldings were added, and Burgundy flags were reinstated on the ground floor. French style dictates that the grammar and vocabulary of architecture are important; aesthetics come before comfort, although there is more than a nod to cosiness and warmth. For this house, the furniture, mirrors and decorative objects were bought from Parisian auction houses, local *brocantes* and provincial antiques shops. Pale pink and yellow pigments were chosen for the walls, and curtains were made of simple checked linen or unlined calico.

91 African farm

When it came to building this new house, surrounded by lush lawns and eucalyptus plantations beside a farm dam in Zimbabwe, the owners were inspired by Australian colonial architecture. With no planning restrictions and an ample supply of home-produced bricks and building timbers, the design could be virtually anything they wanted. They decided on a building only one room wide and extremely long, so that every room faces the water, game park and bush beyond, and with the rooms arranged *en enfilade*, one can see from one end of its immense length to the other. The central entrance hall at the rear, decorated in black, yellow and white, connects through doors, either side of a Jacobean cupboard, to the beamed reception room and on to the full-length covered terraces. The house has only one bedroom (garden cottages accommodate guests) and is entirely on one level. The vast roof is made of a modern, pre-finished corrugated iron, which requires no maintenance. The plastered brick masonry is painted in off-white. This new house works perfectly in the African veld, where the near-perfect climate allows year-round indoor and outdoor living.

92 Cotswold country

The acquisition of a country house is often a tale of falling in love, not something that was difficult in this case, as the location in the Windrush Valley, a short distance from Oxford, is one of the most sought-after in England. The farmhouse, originally a pair of late fifteenth-century cottages, had been enlarged in all directions over the centuries. In the late 1990s it had settled as a rather tired Georgian creation, not without charm, but barely suited to its owner's international lifestyle and business. After a period of getting a feel for the house and its many outbuildings, she asked a local architect, a specialist in heritage work and the local vernacular, to advise on what would become a major transformation. Taking the seventeenth century and the Arts and Crafts movement as their base, they spent four years designing, altering and creating the manor house you can see today. One important factor was the fact that the house should age well. Lime plaster, sawn green oak and reclaimed flagstones immediately changed the interior, along with the sensitive removal of walls, allowing a better use of space. Small rooms and passages were swept away, windows were enlarged or lowered, and a brand-new bedroom wing was added. Opulent fabrics and Asian and specially commissioned furniture combine to create an exceptionally stylish interior.

93 Holiday haven

Near the Cabo de Creus, an hour's drive north of Barcelona, is the fishing village of Cadaqués. The young couple who bought this old house were holidaying from France and decided that it was the ideal place to which to return. The most appealing feature of the house is the way in which it is built into the hillside. It required no structural work, but all the services were renewed, and the owners were left with a blank canvas on which to add colour and texture. Grey, blue, green and yellow colour washes were applied, and previous layers of paint were scraped back to expose past colour schemes in their mottled variations. Since it is a summer holiday home, furnishings were kept simple and inexpensive. Trestle tables, cotton ticking fabrics and market finds from all over Europe fit perfectly into the pretty, rustic interior. As there are no windows at the back of the house, it is cool and dimly lit – the perfect hot-weather retreat.

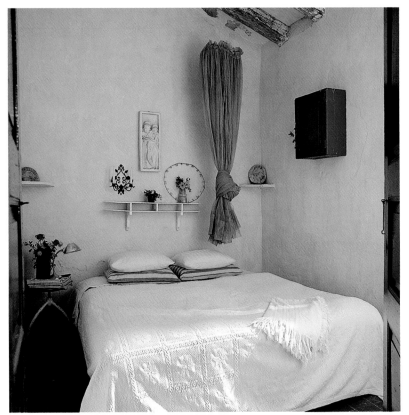

94 Summer hideaway

Major renovation or almost total rebuilding is sometimes required to bring a house up to date and back to life. With a principal residence in Switzerland, the owners of this house near Nice, in the South of France, had spent many happy holidays here, but they decided it needed to be redesigned. A London-based design duo was asked to come up with plans. There were a number of problems associated with the 1930s stone building, and after much discussion it was agreed that the property would be rebuilt. It needed to be enlarged where possible, and a local architect–builder was called in to advise on construction and the supply of correct materials. In order to retain a strong country character, many of the stone walls were left in their natural state; others were just painted, while in some rooms they were both plastered and painted. Structural beams were exposed and the window frames left natural. Outdoor living is an essential part of any holiday home, and in France it is usual to create several shady dining areas, but here cooler evenings have been catered for by building an open-sided pool-house, complete with fireplace. The interiors are furnished with a mix of contemporary and antique furniture and made cosy by the many warm-toned timbers used throughout the house.

95 Burgundian charm

A couple from the Antipodes decided that this French country property near Beaune in Burgundy would be the ideal base for a new life and bed-and-breakfast business, catering to the large number of tourists who visit the region to sample its magnificent wines. The property is entered via a large gate leading into a shady courtyard, the sides of which are formed by buildings each very different architecturally from the others. The house itself is an elegant nineteenth-century residence. Filling another side is a massive and much older wine press. On the third side is a range of barns that the owners have converted into a house for themselves. Park-like gardens embellish the property with majestic trees and provide private places to stroll. The decoration of the house used by guests is traditional and fresh, using pretty cotton fabrics, lacy lampshades and soft pastel colours. Antique chairs and chests, found at various *brocantes* in the area, provide a comfortable family-home feel. Bathrooms are modern and white but include old light fittings and mirrors. Visitors and friends are encouraged to 'put down' wine in the cellar for future visits.

96 Parkland setting

Relocating from the American Midwest, a couple and their two children found a house in Kent, south-east England, with the potential to become a perfect family home. Designed by Decimus Burton and built in 1828, the property has tall, elegant windows, large rooms and – a vital consideration – plenty of wall space on which to hang the owners' collection of modern art. A major refurbishment was undertaken, including the removal of a later extension. With the help of a local interior designer and paint specialist, the interiors began to take shape. A new stone floor was laid in the entrance hall and its walls were given a stone-coloured wash. A similar finish was carried through to the living-room, where a painted coffee table links perfectly with a pair of handmade radiator covers, and a symmetrical arrangement of Donghia sofas and artworks creates a calm, uncluttered atmosphere. Warm yellow was chosen for the dining-room and a blue–green burnished effect for the music room. Black-and-white striped Timney Fowler wallpaper works well in the cloakroom, forming the background to a pair of silhouettes of the couple's daughters. The house has a timeless feel, both architecturally and in the way in which the interiors have been upgraded and carefully decorated.

97 Far pavilion

This gem of a miniature pavilion is one of a pair, set close to the stone boundary walls of a Provençal estate that includes a restored eighteenth-century hunting lodge. Tiny but perfect in its proportions and detailing, it provides a quiet country retreat for a man who works in the frenetic world of international architecture and design. The pavilion contains few rooms – an entrance hall, salon and conservatory-like kitchen on the ground floor, and two bedrooms and a bathroom on the first, the two levels connected by a mahogany spiral staircase – but it nonetheless feels rather special. The setting is sublime and so is the classic French interior. The walls are completely covered in La Toile Villageoise of an old design in madder and cream, which has rapidly become antique in appearance because of the open fire. Tall mirror-panelled cupboards are painted black, as is the specially made kitchen shelving. Black brings weight and balance to many interiors, and is effective here in the white-walled, glass-roofed kitchen. Apart from the piano, brought from the United States, all the contents are French, and most date from the eighteenth and nineteenth centuries, except the charming 1950s Jansen tole table with a tree-trunk base adorned with suitable wildlife.

98 Retiring gracefully

Set on sloping ground below an ancient Provençal village was a small house with poky rooms but astounding views – and the potential to become a perfect year-round home for its new English owners. They realized that they could almost double the size of the residence by removing partition walls and expanding the outdoor living areas. In doing so, they have created an airy, spacious home well suited to the extremes of the local climate. The building is an L-shape, one wing of which houses a large living-room containing a monumental brick-lined fireplace. A small seating area near the entrance marks the boundary of the bedroom wing, which also contains the kitchen and dining-room. The covered veranda overlooking a newly built pool, grassy terraces and an olive grove has far-reaching views across the Lubéron plain. Most of the furnishings came from the owners' previous home in England. White sofas and chairs are grouped on a limited-edition rug by Gillian Ayres; a collection of 1950s signed Daum glass and a magnificent 1940s Murano glass ceiling light add shimmer to the living-room; and a collection of artwork by Anne Pourny and Francesca Chandon brings vivid colour to the white-painted walls.

99 Country life

This pretty country house is located in Oxfordshire, central England, in an area of outstanding beauty, both natural and man-made. Built of chalk and fossil limestone in the late seventeenth century, it was part of a large estate for nearly 300 years and remained until recently largely unmodernized. It is a traditional 'longhouse', meaning that there are no wasted spaces where corridors lead from one room to another: from the kitchen at one end there is an *enfilade* view through the rooms to the living-room at the opposite end. The owner, a designer who trained with the famous firm of Colefax and Fowler, carried out a sensitive restoration, carefully preserving the many original elements both inside and out. She chose the decoration to complement the wonderful old tile, stone and timber floors, the surviving Jacobean panelling and the rather grander fireplaces than would usually be found in such a house. Fabrics were bought from Robert Kime, Braquenié, and Colefax and Fowler, the colours ranging from deep reds and soft pinks to warm yellows and limestone. The bedrooms are paler and lighter, using grey–greens and soft blues – restful colours that work particularly well in country houses.

100 Simply country

Approached across a beautifully planted enclosed courtyard, this U-shaped house in the South of France looks completely different from the side, appearing to have grown straight from a field. It is the last of a tiny group of farmhouses in an *hameau* (hamlet), clustered together in an undulating landscape of fields and orchards. The owner, a landscape gardener and author, undertook the design himself, carrying out major work to create a family home; at the same time, he found that the space in one of the wings proved ideal as offices. The layout of the rooms is excellent. The central portion of the ground floor encompasses the dining-room and kitchen, with a modern staircase in between, while the living-room spreads across the first floor. Bedrooms and bathrooms are situated in each of the wings. By keeping to a pure-white colour scheme and revealing all the ceiling beams, the owner has rendered the interiors fresh and bright. No effort was made to attempt a Provençal look: instead, modern sofas are mixed with the odd antique, artwork is contemporary, and there is an uncluttered simplicity throughout the house.

Credits

1 Design: Jean-Louis Raynaud and Kenyon Kramer, Decoration-Jardin, 3 Place des Ormeaux, 13100 Aix-en-Provence, France; +33 (0)4 42 23 52 32.

2 Design: Annie Constantine; annieabfab@aol.com. Feature originally produced by Sally Griffiths.

3 Design: Alexandra Stoddard; alexandrastoddard.com. Feature originally produced by Amanda Harling.

4 Design: Sally Jeeves.

5 Design: John Leaning.

6 Design: Isabelle de Borchgrave; isabelledeborchgrave.com.

7 Design: Jean-Louis Raynaud, Decoration-Jardin, 3 Place des Ormeaux, 13100 Aix-en-Provence, France; +33 (0)4 42 23 52 32.

8 Design: Marc Johnson. Feature originally sourced and produced by Amanda Harling.

9 Design: Anne Millais, Millais Interior Design; +44 (0)1869 350951. Feature originally produced by Amanda Harling.

10 Design: Charlotte Smith. Feature originally produced by Sally Griffiths.

11 Owner: Nina Bahmatova.

12 Architecture/restoration: Bureau d'Études Bruno & Alexandre Lafourcade, 10 Boulevard Victor Hugo, 13210 Saint-Rémy-de-Provence, France; architecture-lafourcade.com.

13 Design: Jenny Uglow.

14 Owner/design: Frank Faulkner. Feature originally sourced and produced by Victoria Ahmadi.

16 Design: Robert Hering.

17 Architecture: Harry Scott. Design: Sophie Ryder and Harry Scott. Art: second page: portrait above fireplace by Joseph Tonneau, animal sculpture by Sophie Ryder; third page: work seen through door by Francis Holl.

18 Design: Jorn Langberg. Feature originally sourced and produced by Sally Griffiths.

19 Architecture/build: David Price Design; davidpricedesign.com. Design: Victoria Waymouth.

20 Design: Freya Swaffer, Spencer Swaffer Antiques, 30 High Street, Arundel, West Sussex BN18 9AB; spencerswaffer.com.

21 Owner/design: Hannes Myburgh, Meerlust Estate, Stellenbosch, South Africa.

22 Architecture/restoration: Bureau d'Études Bruno & Alexandre Lafourcade, 10 Boulevard Victor Hugo, 13210 Saint-Rémy-de-Provence, France; architecture-lafourcade.com. Specialist decorative painter: Lucinda Oakes; oakesart@btinternet.com.

23 Design: Mary Rose Young, ceramicist; maryroseyoung.com. Feature originally sourced and produced by Heidede Carstensen. Pictures courtesy of EWA Associates.

24 Design: Pauline Mann.

25 Architecture: Wolf Siegfried Wagner. Design: Nona von Haeften. Feature originally sourced and produced by Amanda Harling.

26 Design: Bettina von Bülow.

27 Design: Avril Delahunt, Delahunt Designs; +33 (0)5 53 20 99 94; auvergnats1@aol.com. Feature originally produced by Amanda Harling.

28 Design: Catharine Warren-Geist.

29 Design: Axel Vervoordt, Kasteel van 's-Gravenwezel, St.-Jobsteenweg 64, 2970 's-Gravenwezel, Belgium; +32 (0)3 680 14 89; axel-vervoordt.com. Feature originally produced by Sally Griffiths.

30 Design: Carrie Barlow; barlowmail@btinternet.com. Feature originally produced by Amanda Harling.

31 Owner: Craig Barnard; thebodyholiday.com. Design: Penny Barnard. Feature originally sourced and produced by Amanda Harling; subsequent feature produced by Sally Griffiths.

32 Design: Stephen and Luisella Barrow.

33 Owner: Ludmilla Tatianina.

34 Design: Monique Waqué; +49 (0)173 240 52 53.

35 Design: Roland Lebevillon and Maurice Savinel. Feature originally produced by Sally Griffiths.

36 Architecture: Wolf Siegfried Wagner. Design: Nona von Haeften. Feature originally sourced and produced by Amanda Harling.

37 Design: Lesley Cooke, Lesley Cooke Design; lesley@chezcooke.com.

38 Design: Anne Grafton. Feature originally sourced and produced by Pattie Barron.

39 Design: Barbara Ther.

40 Design: Nick Etherington-Smith.

41 Design: Konrad and Fiona Adamczewsky. Feature originally produced by Rose Hammick.

42 Owner/design: Monsieur Antonin.

43 Design: Jaine McCormack and Robert Barber. Feature originally produced by Mary Gilliatt.

44 Architecture/restoration: Bureau d'Études Bruno & Alexandre Lafourcade, 10 Boulevard Victor Hugo, 13210 Saint-Rémy-de-Provence, France; architecture-lafourcade.com.

45 Design: Keith Skeel, Keith Skeel Antiques & Eccentricities, Loudham Hall, Pettistree, Woodbridge, Suffolk IP13 0NN; +44 (0)1728 745900; keithskeel.com. Feature originally produced by Amanda Harling.

46 Design: Gilles Vuillemard.

47 Design: Annie Constantine; annieabfab@aol.com.

48 Design: Anne Fischer, Fischer Wohnen; +49 (0)2525 9 52 11 0; fischer-wohnen.com. Feature originally produced by Victoria Ahmadi.

49 Design: Elizabeth Gage; +44 (0)20 7823 0100; eg@elizabeth-gage.com; elizabeth-gage.com. Feature originally produced by Sally Griffiths.

50 Design: Leif Pedersen and Fiona S. Graham; lamaisondelahalle.com. Feature originally produced by Amanda Harling.

51 Design: Anne Millais, Millais Interior Design; +44 (0)1869 350951. Feature originally sourced and produced by Amanda Harling.

52 Refurbishment/design: Jean-Louis Raynaud and Kenyon Kramer, Decoration-Jardin, 3 Place des Ormeaux, 13100 Aix-en-Provence, France; +33 (0)4 42 23 52 32.

53 Architecture (alterations): Christopher Smallwood.

54 Design: Jean-Louis Raynaud and Kenyon Kramer, Decoration-Jardin, 3 Place des Ormeaux, 13100 Aix-en-Provence, France; +33 (0)4 42 23 52 32.

55 Design: Juliet de Valero Wills, Design Dorset.

56 Design: Frédéric Méchiche. Feature originally produced by Sally Griffiths.

57 Design: Joan Brendle. Feature originally produced by Amanda Harling.

58 Design: Simon Munn and Lesley Hall, Munn & Hall Associates, The Old Mill, Old Mill Lane, Sheet, Hampshire GU31 4DA; +44 (0)1730 268296. Feature originally produced by Amanda Harling.

59 Design: Yavuz Karaözbek and Patrick Just.

60 Design: Inge Sprawson. Feature originally produced by Amanda Harling.

61 Design: Sophie Stonor-von Hirsch; sophie@stonor.com.

62 Design: William Thuillier, 14 Old Bond Street, London W1X 3DB;

+44 (0)20 7499 0106; thuillart.com. Feature originally produced by Amanda Harling.

63 Design: Holger Stewen, Holger Stewen Interior Design, Calle de Santo Domingo 12, 07001 Palma, Mallorca; +34 (0)971 727016; holgerstewen.com. Feature originally sourced and produced by Victoria Ahmadi.

64 Design: Henry and Athena Strutt and David Price Design; davidpricedesign.com.

65 Design: Alison Sloga, Garden Whisperer; alison@gardenwhisperer.com. Feature originally produced by Amanda Harling.

66 Design: Sylvia Napier; sylvia@napier1939.fsnet.co.uk.

67 Design: Birdie Fortescue; +44 (0)1206 337557; birdiefortescue.com.

68 Architecture/design: Lachlan and Annie Stewart, ANTA; anta.co.uk.

69 Architecture/design: Bureau d'Études Bruno & Alexandre Lafourcade, 10 Boulevard Victor Hugo, 13210 Saint-Rémy-de-Provence, France; architecture-lafourcade.com.

70 Owners: Fiona and David Mellor. Design: David Mellor; davidmellordesign.com.

71 Design: Nicky Dingwall-Main.

72 Design: Dörte Wehmeyer, An Den Kastanien 1, 50859 Cologne, Germany; +49 (0)221 5 00 22 04. Feature originally sourced and produced by Amanda Harling.

73 Design: Daniel Dufour; la-cabane-perchee.com. Feature originally produced by Sabine Wesemann.

74 Design: Julia Langton; +44 (0)1793 814950; burderop@ukonline.co.uk. Feature originally produced by Amanda Harling.

75 Owners: Mr and Mrs Pieter van Naeltwijck. Architecture: Bureau d'Études Bruno & Alexandre Lafourcade, 10 Boulevard Victor Hugo, 13210 Saint-Rémy-de-

Provence, France; architecture-lafourcade.com.

76 Design: Holger Stewen, Holger Stewen Interior Design, Calle de Santo Domingo 12, 07001 Palma, Mallorca; +34 (0)971 727016; holgerstewen.com. Feature originally produced by Amanda Harling.

77 Owners: Clare and Mark Hanson. Design: Hanson Interiors.

78 Design: French Country Living; +33 (0)613 237 084; frenchcountrylivingantiques.com.

79 Design: Constanze von Unruh, Constanze Interior Projects Ltd. Feature originally produced by Amanda Harling.

80 Design: Niels Hansen and Steffen Reimers, Marché Noir; +49 (0)40 27 88 22 72; marche-noir.de. Feature originally produced by Victoria Ahmadi.

81 Design: Penny Morrison, Morrison Interiors; +44 (0)1547 560460; penny@pennymorrison.com.

82 Design: Lara Fawcett. Feature originally produced by Heather Dixon.

83 Design: Julia Morison.

84 Design: Matthew and Miranda Eden.

85 Design: Hugh and Jane Faulkner; grandcros.fr.

86 Design: Toni Muntaner, Mallorca. Feature originally sourced and produced by Amanda Harling.

87 Design: Hugo Grenville; hugogrenville.com. Feature originally produced by Amanda Harling.

88 Owner/design: Ginny Magher, Ginny Magher Interiors; ginny@gmagher.com. Architecture/restoration: Bureau d'Études Bruno & Alexandre Lafourcade, 10 Boulevard Victor Hugo, 13210 Saint-Rémy-de-Provence, France; architecture-lafourcade.com.

89 Design: Giles Vincent and Nigel Pearce, Giles Vincent Design Associates; +44 (0)20 7917 1826. Feature originally produced by Sally Griffiths.

90 Design: Gerard Conway; +44 (0)7875 602198, +33 (0)631 822 965; gerard@gerardconway.com.

91 Owners/design: Carol and Ian Gordon.

92 Design: Alison Henry, Alison Henry Ltd; info@alisonhenry.com.

93 Design: Anders and Tami Christiansen. Feature originally sourced by Sally Griffiths.

94 Architecture/design: Collett-Zarzycki in collaboration with Robert Dallas; collett-zarzycki.com. Feature originally produced by Heidede Carstensen.

95 Design: Bruce and Ann Leonard.

96 Design: Michael Daly; md@michaeldalydesign.com. Feature originally produced by Amanda Harling.

97 Architecture/design: Kenyon Kramer and Jean-Louis Raynaud, Decoration-Jardin, 3 Place des Ormeaux, 13100 Aix-en-Provence, France; +33 (0)4 42 23 52 32.

98 Design: Annabel Beauchamp.

99 Design: Nikki Atkinson, Nikki Atkinson Ltd; +44 (0)844 700 8011; nikkiatkinson@aol.com.

100 Design: Alex Dingwall-Main; +33 (0)4 90 75 86 34; alex@admgarden.com.

Acknowledgements

Andreas von Einsiedel would like to thank warmly the producers of the features and the many owners, designers and architects featured in this book.

First published 2009 by Merrell Publishers Limited

81 Southwark Street
London SE1 0HX

merrellpublishers.com

Photography copyright © 2009 Andreas von Einsiedel
Text, design and layout copyright © 2009 Merrell
Publishers Limited

All rights reserved. No part of this publication may be
reproduced, stored in a retrieval system or transmitted,
in any form or by any means, electronic, mechanical,
photocopying, recording or otherwise, without the prior
written permission of the publisher.

British Library Cataloguing-in-Publication Data:
Einsiedel, Andreas
Dream homes country : 100 inspirational interiors
1. Country homes – Decoration 2. Country homes –
Decoration – Pictorial works 3. Interior decoration
4. Interior decoration – Pictorial works
I. Title II. Thornycroft, Johanna
747'.091734

ISBN 978-1-8589-4474-6

Produced by Merrell Publishers Limited
Design concept by Martin Lovelock
Layout by Paul Shinn
Copy-edited by Henrietta Heald, Helen Miles
and Kirsty Seymour-Ure
Proof-read by Elizabeth Tatham
Printed and bound in China

Front jacket: project no. 97
Back jacket: project no. 55
Frontispiece: project no. 85
Dedication: project no. 34
Introduction images: project nos. 88 and 41